THE ILLUSTRATED GUIDE TO
HORSES
OF THE WORLD

THE ILLUSTRATED GUIDE TO
HORSES
OF THE WORLD

Caroline Silver

Illustrations by Ko van den Broecke, with
additional illustrations by Sean Milne

LONGMEADOW
P R E S S

First published in Great Britain by Elsevier Phaidon
(an imprint of Phaidon Press Limited)

© 1976 Andromeda Oxford Ltd

ISBN 0 681 41894 X

Printed in Singapore by Tien Wah Press

First Longmeadow Press Edition 1993

Reprinted 1994, 1995

09876543

CONTENTS

LIST OF BREEDS

HORSES: WARM-BLOODED

7

THE HISTORY OF THE HORSE

The history of the horse begins in the Lower Eocene period, 55 million years ago, when the continental land masses, the mountain ranges, and the Atlantic and Indian oceans began to form. In this epoch the Rocky Mountains, the Andes, the Alps and the Panama Ridge took shape and the Gulf Stream began its thermal control of Europe's weather. During this time marine reptiles became extinct, placental mammals evolved, and on land there began to appear the ancestors of the elephant, the rhinoceros, the ox, the pig, the monkey, and the horse.

The horse in its earliest form, some 50 million years before man evolved, was a very small multi-toed mammal called *Hyracotherium*. The name is derived, rather confusingly, from the Greek word for hog. *Hyracotherium* was about 12in tall. It had four toes on its forefeet and three on its hind, and during its evolution through the Middle Eocene, Oligocene, Miocene and Pliocene epochs – a long, slow jump of 66 million years – the fourth toe on the forefoot disappeared, the center of the three remaining toes developed into a rudimentary hoof, and the outer toes shrank into vestigial appendages that no longer reached the ground.

The vast number of *Hyracotherium* bones that fossil seekers find in their digs among the soil and rock of the southern United States is reasonable proof that today's extensively subdivided family of hoofed mammals originated on that side of the world. Migrating northward they wandered into Asia and Europe, crossing land that had not yet subsided into the waters of the arctic regions, and thereafter the American and Eurasian branches of the family followed very different courses to extinction. *Hyracotherium* died out some 40 million years ago, having failed to adapt itself to changing geological conditions. It was succeeded by *Orohippus* and subsequently by *Epihippus*, animals with very similar skeletal structure but with increasingly efficient teeth. In *Pliohippus* of the Lower Pliocene period a fully-hoofed

11

animal three times the size of *Hyracotherium* emerged, an animal which by the time *Homo sapiens* began had developed into *Equus* and had grown in stature to about 13 hands (52in) high.

Like *Hyracotherium, Equus* seems to have originated in North America; unlike *Hyracotherium*, it migrated southward and became South America's earliest horse. It also spread to Asia, expanded into Europe, and from there went south to Africa. About 8,000 years ago it became extinct in the Americas; and the adapted types of Europe, Asia and Africa — different species of *Equus* emerged according to terrain and climate — became the exclusive ancestors of the modern horse.

The ancestral types

Three basic ancestors, the Steppe, the Forest, and the Plateau horses of prehistory, are widely supposed to have been responsible for the huge variety of *Equus caballus* of today, though conflicting evidence from expert sources shows that there are no certainties even in the comparatively recent origins of the modern world; and, since one of the characteristics of *Equus* is that all varieties of it can interbreed, it is reasonable to suppose that cross-breds and variations of these types existed long before man interfered with breeding for selected qualities. The Steppe type had a large head with long ears, a convex profile and a very long face. Its body was short and strong, supported on slender limbs with long, narrow hooves. Its mane stood straight up, brush-like, on a thick neck. Its color was probably dun with black points, with zebra markings on its legs and a stripe on its shoulder. It would have had a pronounced donkey-stripe down its back. It was alert, agile, ready to scramble over most obstacles, and would enter water without fear. Remnants of it exist today, apparently unaltered, in *Equus Przewalskii Przewalskii Poliakov*, otherwise known as Przewalski's Horse or the wild horse of Mongolia (see page 79).

The Forest type, stupider and heavier than the Steppe, is thought to be the ancestor of most of the "cold-blooded" heavy horses of today. It was strong and thickly-built, with a long body on short, strong legs ending in broad, rounded hooves suitable for walking on marshy ground without sinking in up to its elbows. It had a broad, short head, concave between the eyes and convex towards the muzzle, which made it comparatively easy for it to eat young shoots and the bark of trees and which gave it a faintly elk-like appearance. It had a long mane and a thick, low-set tail, and its basic

The illustrations opposite show the main lines of survival of the horse up to 7 million years ago. Many other variations died out through failure to adapt. Hyracotherium (1), just as well known by the name Eohippus, the "dawn horse", differs so much from what we know today as a horse that when its remnants were first discovered in the 19th century it was not recognized as a horse at all. Mesohippus (2), of the Oligocene period, was a 3-toed browser; and by the time of the Miocene epoch it had evolved into Mery-chippus (3), a 3-toed grazer with longer grinding teeth. Pliohippus (4), the first 1-toed grazer had even longer teeth.

4 · PLIOHIPPUS

3 · MERYCHIPPUS

PARAHIPPUS

MIOHIPPUS

2 · MESOHIPPUS

EPIHIPPUS

OROHIPPUS

1 · HYRACOTHERIUM

color was a dark dun, often with stripes or spots which helped to conceal it in the dappled shadows of the forest. It had a pronounced fear of water, no doubt because the trees overhanging a forest watering place provided ideal ambushes for the horse's predators.

The Plateau type is still just about extant in the few remaining herds of Tarpan (*Equus Przewalskii Gmelini Ant.*), though it should be pointed out that the last official Tarpan died in 1887 and that what is today called Tarpan was rounded up from Polish peasants whose animals appeared, but were never proved, to be Tarpan in every way. It has a small, narrow head with small ears, large eyes, a straight or concave face — altogether a much finer look about it than the Forest or the Steppe types. Its body is lighter in weight, its limbs comparatively long and slender, and its hooves midway between the long narrowness of the Steppe and the round broadness of the Forest. It has abundant mane and tail, and is dun-colored with dark points, a donkey-stripe down its back, and sometimes stripes on the forelegs and inner thighs (see page 85). This Plateau horse is very probably the ancestor of today's lightweight ponies and of our finer-built horses.

The development of the modern horse

None of the ancient types of horse were "horses" by today's definition, which is one of height rather than of type. A horse is an animal standing more than 14.2 hands high (58in) at the withers, the highest point of the back. Anything less than this height is a pony. (Hands are so-called because the height was originally measured in clenched fists placed one on top of the other, and the average measure of a man's fist is four inches.) The increased stature of the horse, along with many other refinements, seems to have started with primitive man who, once he had the knowledge and the facilities to keep alive the wild horses he caught, must soon have become trapped in the greatest of all horse problems man has ever given himself to cope with: how to improve what he had for his own specific purposes.

The primitive pony types must have had a hard time of it in their first relations with man. Initially the ponies who were caught would have been the sick and the lame, the very young and the very stupid. These were no doubt hobbled or tethered in the most primitive fashion and fed on fodder that was inadequate, resulting in starvation and deformity of breed. Horses depended, and depend, on a variation of diet that is inadequately met by even the most superb grass, and it is beyond doubt that only unlimited range, not richness of pasture, kept the wild herds alive.

Taking what he had or had heard of, man inbred or outcrossed for speed, for strength, for endurance, for size, for sweetness of nature, for hardiness, for beauty, for athletic ability, until today there are a great many "breeds" on record (though some are so alike that they are indistinguishable). The range of size and ability is enormous, stretching from the huge Shire, the biggest horse in the world, which is often so tall that a man cannot see over its back, to the tiny Shetland pony, the smallest recorded specimen of which was only 6.2hh (26in), and the dog-sized Falabella. The Shire, traditionally evolved from the medieval Great Horse of Britain who carried

The Steppe type

The Forest type

The war horse of the middle ages

armored knights into battle, has become the perfect draught horse, combining a docile nature with stamina and great strength; yet comparatively it is not as strong as the Shetland, which, for its size, is considered the strongest of all breeds. The Shetland can pull twice its own weight, which makes it twice as strong as most of the heavy breeds, and a 9hh Shetland is recorded (1820) as having carried a 170-lb man 40 miles in one day. The Shetland's strength has astounded many visitors to its native habitat. Writing in 1701 in his *Brief Description of Orkney, Zetland, Pightland-Firth and Caithness*, the Reverend John Brand had this to say:

They have a sort of little Horses called Shelties, than which no other are to be had, if not brought thither, from other places, they are of less size than the Orkney Horses, for some will be but 9 or 10 Nevis or Handbreadths high, and they will be thought big horses there if eleven, and although so small they are full of vigour and life, and . . . Summer or Winter they never come into an House but run upon the Mountains in some places as flocks, and if at any time in the Winter the storm be so great, that they are straightened for food, they will come down from the Hills when the Ebb is in the sea, and eat the Sea-Ware (as likewise do the sheep) . . .

The Coldness of the Air, the Barrenness of the Mountains on which they feed and their hard usage may occasion them to keep so little, for if bigger Horses be brought into the Country, their kind within a little time will degenerate; and indeed in the present case we may see the Wisdome of Providence, for their way being deep and Mossie in many places, these lighter Horses come through when the greater and heavier would sink down; and they leap over ditches very nimbly; yea up and down Mossy braes and Hillocks with heavy riders upon them, which I could not look upon but with Admiration, yea I have seen them climb up braes upon their knees, when otherwise they could not get the height overcome, so that our Horses would be but little if at all serviceable there.

Other selected qualities have produced other astonishing breeds of *Equus*. For example, the hardy, desert-bred Arabian, which is beyond compare for endurance. During the Crimean War a bay stallion named Omar Pasha carried a dispatch rider the 93 miles from Silistra to Varna at high speed to bring news of the Russian repulse. The rider delivered his message and fell dead of exhaustion, but his Arab mount seemed as fresh as ever.

The creation of the Thoroughbred

The speed with which selective breeding for a particular quality can be brought into effect can be seen from a comparison of the English Thoroughbred with its ancestor the Arabian. The Thoroughbred, bred solely for speed, had its inception in James I's attempts to keep his hot-headed Scottish nobles out of trouble by introducing racing at his hunting lodge in the little village of Newmarket. James imported Oriental stock and bred it onto the fastest of the local mares, but it was not until the end of the 17th and the beginning of the 18th century that the three great foundation stallions from which all Thoroughbreds are descended were put to work in earnest to start the Thoroughbred racehorse. All three stallions were Arabians. In 1793 Thoroughbreds were for the first time recorded as a breed in the General Stud Book, which starts with a list of 100 Oriental stallions and 43 part-bred Oriental mares; and in its issue of 4 April 1842 the magazine *Hippologische Blaetter* recorded a trial between Arabs and Thoroughbreds which had taken place only a quarter of a century after the founding of the G.S.B.:

About 1815 or 1820, when Kurshid Pasha was governor of the Nejd, some Englishmen who had brought Thoroughbreds out with them, proposed to race against the Arabs; this was agreed, only the English asked for a delay of forty days in order to get their horses in condition. The Arabs, whose racehorses are always fit, did not know what they meant, but agreed to the delay, and the meeting took place on the agreed day. The Arabs asked the English to choose which horses were to race, and inquired how many days the race was to last. Now it was the English who were astonished, and they answered, "Our races only last an hour." Whereupon the Bedouin burst out laughing, being of the opinion it was not worth the trouble of training a horse for forty days and then only running for an hour. But as the

English explained, this was their custom at home, and after such training they would beat the Arabs as they had beaten all other Europeans.

The Bedouin laughed again; but when two animals enveloped in felt from top to toe, led by two miserable creatures hardly recognizable as men – the English grooms – appeared, they laughed even louder at the long-legged gaunt creatures and thought they were being made fun of, and it took all the persuasive powers of Kurshid Pasha, who was present, to get them to run at all. While a skinny stable lad was mounting his equally emaciated steed, a stocky Bedouin, lance in hand, swung into the saddle of his normal-sized mount.

It was agreed to race for three hours, and at a given signal they started. After the first half-hour the English were leading, but the Nejdis soon caught up with them, at last passing them, so that the English passed the post a long time after the Arabs. The English horses were winded and stood stock still, while the Nejdis were still gay, stamping the ground and challenging their opponents to a further match. As for the Arab riders, they shrugged their shoulders over a horse that is not fit to gallop on after only three hours.

Thus horses bred for speed from stock bred for endurance failed in a very short span of years to have any comparison in what was, by today's standards, strictly an endurance test. Today, breeding for speed has so far outdistanced breeding for stamina in the Thoroughbred that it is unthinkable that he should be asked to race for one hour, let alone for three. On the other hand his Arab forebears would have no chance with him on the racecourse: the fastest British time recorded at Epsom, a very fast track for the shorter races, is that of Indigenous, who in 1960 went 5 furlongs carrying 131 lb in 53.6 seconds, an average of just over 42mph – and no Arab could live with that.

Horses have been bred, of course, for reasons other than strength or speed. The greatest refinement of the horse, which embodies to the full its intelligent ability to respond to the wishes of a man, is shown in the amazing manoeuver of the trained Lipizzaner stallion that is called the *capriole* (see illustration page 145). In the capriole the horse leaps vertically from a standing start to the height of a man, kicks out with its hind legs, and descends with its feet more or less on the same spot where it started. It is a breathtaking display of cooperation between horse and rider which is well justified today purely as a spectacle of horsemanship; but the capriole originated as a battle manoeuver to gain clearance for a rider surrounded by enemies, and as such it must have been a formidable weapon of war.

The pedigreed breeds

The division of horses into pedigreed breeds is mostly a thing of modern times. During the Middle Ages you got about on indeterminate types such as the *haquenai* (the medieval equivalent of the bicycle) if you were very poor, or such as the palfrey (sports car) if you were richer and flashier. "Breeds" of horses, all descended from the same mixed stock, came to be widespread first for commercial purposes when communications improved to the extent that a whole nation could learn the advantages of possessing a certain type of horse for a specific function, and were therefore encouraged to ask for proof of "the real thing", and secondly — and only very recently — because people were given the opportunity, through the development of motorization, to regard the horse not as a working animal but as a luxury object to have around the place *only because they liked him*. Tracing the pedigree of any given animal back over a century or more, one runs invariably into the equivalent of "by Squire Thorner's black out of Farmer Jones's good mare"; before this it is only guesswork, and before guesswork lie the primitive prehistoric types from which all horses trace and from which the modern breeds must descend.

Therefore it must be obvious that the modern breeds of horse and pony begin and end in the middle; that new ones are evolving, and that established ones may not continue. In trying to list all, or most, of the breeds of horse and pony the question that continually arises is, "When is a breed not a breed?" The answer may be, "When it hasn't got a Breed Society."

Today's horse is almost universally a thing of people's leisure time. But the function does not matter; the reason for the continued existence of the horse is unimportant. What is important, to the millions who appreciate this very special kind of animal, is that the horse, no matter how indefinite its future shape or purpose, is here, and always will be.

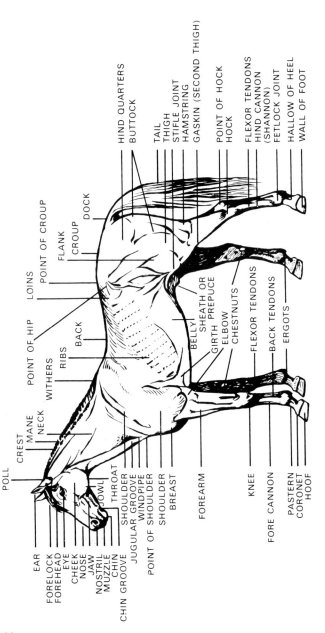

POINTS OF THE HORSE

POLL

CREST
MANE
NECK

POINT OF HIP
POINT OF CROUP

LOINS
POINT OF CROUP
FLANK
CROUP
DOCK

HIND QUARTERS
BUTTOCK

TAIL
THIGH
STIFLE JOINT
HAMSTRING
GASKIN (SECOND THIGH)

POINT OF HOCK
HOCK

FLEXOR TENDONS
HIND CANNON (SHANNON)
FETLOCK JOINT
HALLOW OF HEEL
WALL OF FOOT

WITHERS
POINT OF HIP
RIBS
BACK

BELLY
SHEATH OR GIRTH PREPUCE
ELBOW
CHESTNUTS
FLEXOR TENDONS
BACK TENDONS
ERGOTS

EAR
FORELOCK
FOREHEAD
EYE
CHEEK
NOSE
JAW
NOSTRIL
MUZZLE
CHIN
CHIN GROOVE
JOWL
THROAT
SHOULDER
JUGULAR GROOVE
WINDPIPE
POINT OF SHOULDER
SHOULDER
BREAST

FOREARM

KNEE

FORE CANNON

PASTERN
CORONET
HOOF

20

BUYING
A HORSE

This section is intended for the amateur enthusiast who wants a riding horse or pony. It does not include suggestions for those who want, for example, to build up a stud or watch their horses win on the racetrack, since such people, if not already expert themselves, will be employing specialist advice.

Buying a good horse is easy. Go to the biggest horse shows in the country and buy a horse that wins consistently. It will cost far more than it can ever make in prize money, and in all probability it will depreciate in value at a speed that even the rashest investor would not entertain. For the not-so-rich amateur who wants a reasonable animal at a fair price it's a little more complicated.

Horses are relatively difficult to assess both in price and suitability. Unlike a used car a horse has no fixed value, so price depends upon the eagerness of the buyer and current market competition. Fashions in some types of horse – children's ponies are an excellent example – can be as wayward and changeable as fashions in clothes (and frequently much less meaningful). So if everyone is after a palomino, for instance, it may be possible to buy the same number in bay at half the cost. More obviously, colts and mares suitable for stud are likely to have a higher price tag than geldings. Though it by no means follows that an unfashionable color or sex is necessarily a bargain it is often worth enquiring about, because if the buyer does not actually save money he at least learns more about the breed he wants.

Suitability of a horse depends upon the proficiency of the rider, on the age, size, strength and ability of the horse, and on its health and character (not to mention the rider's). Suiting horse to rider is best done abstractly, before any specific horse is considered for purchase. The horse needs to be big and strong enough to carry the rider comfortably, but not too big and strong for the rider to control. It should be capable of living under conditions that its owner can easily provide – that is, there is no point, if the rider lives in a cold climate, in buying a thin-skinned Thoroughbred if he cannot afford stabling, blankets, oats and two or three hours a day of care and exercise.

The horse must be sound for the purposes for which it will be used. A horse that is unsound in wind, for example, might run out of breath during a fox hunt but could be perfectly fine for hacking.

Since so much time has to be spent with a horse it is important that the owner should *like* the animal. Taking a liking to a particular horse is as immediate and as positive as a reaction to a new face at a party. Expect no similar reaction from the horse, since his initial response is invariably one of indifference until he has had a few weeks' experience of a new owner; but the undercurrent of sympathy and trust which to many is the most pleasant part of owning a horse cannot evolve unless at least one side of the partnership is predisposed towards it.

Questions to ask oneself before buying a horse:

What do you want to use it for?

Where will you keep it? Will restrictions of stabling, grazing, or budget eliminate types of horses you might otherwise consider buying?

Have you enough time to look after it (estimate two hours a day; more for stable-kept horses)? Alternatively, can you get someone to look after it for you? Who will look after it when you are away from home?

Is the area you live in really suitable for riding? Do local conditions (rough terrain, heavy traffic) in any way define the type of horse you should have?

Are there enough diverse places to ride to keep you happy for 365 days of the year?

Are you fond enough of riding to spend necessary time with your horse in the foulest weather of the year?

What is the maximum you are willing to pay? (It is never a good idea to economize on the purchase price, as a cheaper animal with a flaw in temperament or physique will in the long run cost much more than the saving on the purchase price.)

Answers to questions such as these help to define the horse required, and indeed to define whether a horse is required at all. If what is the ideal horse is understood in advance then the risk of buying a charming but unsuitable animal is much cut down. The temptation to buy a beautiful, though impractical, horse is enormous when the animal is before your eyes. Only by knowing precisely what is wanted and being patient until the right horse comes up for sale can the perfect horse be acquired.

A horse is an athlete, and should look like one. Here are a few points to look for in a riding horse or pony:

Head: Alert and proudly held, not over-large. A riding animal with a heavy head will be heavy on the reins.

Eyes: Large and intelligent. Kind horses have kindly eyes. Piggy little eyes reveal piggy little natures. Stick a finger almost into each eye to see if it blinks. If it doesn't, it is blind. Potentially a horse can suffer from as many vision deficiences as a human, and bad sight can make it shy at phantoms for which its rider will not be prepared.

Withers: Prominent, and back not too fat — otherwise the saddle will slip forwards or sideways.

Legs: Smooth and cool to the touch. A horse whose legs are scarred and bumpy, if not actually unsound, will certainly be careless. Have it trotted towards you and away. If its feet swing out sideways, or alternatively if it almost crosses them over, avoid it. Don't buy it if it shuffles.

Pasterns: Strong and springy. If nearly vertical ("upright") they will get jarred trotting on roads.

Feet: Round and neat. If they are splayed, uneven, split, or cracked – especially if cracked from the top of the hoof down – don't buy it.

Wind: Unsoundness such as roaring or whistling is particularly difficult to detect. Easier to hear if you can get someone to gallop the horse past you. Everyone will hear it when you have it in the hunting field.

Coughing: If the horse coughs, even once, don't buy it. It may well be only a bit of dust in its throat, but it could also be a sign of serious illness.

Unless the horse is to be stabled all the time, ask to see it caught (animals which are hard to catch become a daily nightmare). Have it walked and trotted past you, towards you and away from you, to see if it carries itself well, has a nice springy stride, and if its action is straight. Saddle it up yourself to see if it is well-behaved. Mount it and walk, trot and canter it. Put it over a small jump. Test it in traffic (safer to lead it, in case it fails). If you like it and take it home, allow time for it to settle down. Moving is traumatic for a horse. Until it knows you and comes to meet you, leave a headcollar on it in the field with 12in of rope attached to catch it by.

Naturally enough, a good, experienced horse is nearly always expensive, though some saving can be made if it is bought at the least useful time of year. Thus bargains in show horses mainly happen at the end of the showing season. A cheap hunter is easiest to find when hunting finishes and hunt stables and private owners sell off horses they do not want to keep through the summer. Thoroughbreds can sometimes be had quite cheaply at race-horse sales when racing stables throw out their disappointing runners, but unless the buyer has inside knowledge such horses may well turn out to be unsound, and the purchaser must anyway provide expert care and handling if the horse is to be transformed into a good riding animal.

For children, who are often capable of enthusiastic neglect, the wisest buys are native ponies or cross-breds, since these are naturally adapted to the climate and will live outdoors quite happily all year if given a shelter of some kind, and of course additional feed when the grass dies down in winter. A pony for a child should be sensible and kind. Ponies aged between seven and ten are the most in demand because they are old enough to be steady but have not yet begun to show signs of wear. But much older ponies should not be rejected solely on the grounds of age. Provided it's healthy and up to work, an experienced old pony is an excellent teacher.

Buying your favorite animal from the local riding stable can be a mistake because you know it only as a hard-working member of a herd (horses behave better in company). By itself and lightly worked it may be a brute. Advertisements can also be a let-down, since it may mean traveling miles only to find that what the advertiser thinks is a beauty is, in your opinion, a wretch. Horse sales, for the casual buyer with no inside connections, are best avoided altogether because there is no opportunity to try the animal out. The safest way to buy a horse is to get one you know and like from a friend. Failing that, a reputable dealer (one who's been in business for some time in the same locality) is always willing to find you a suitable horse if he knows what you want and how much you are prepared to pay. Try it out, and buy it "subject to veterinary examination" so that if your veterinary surgeon objects to it you can send it back. Always choose the vet yourself, making sure that he is one who specializes in horses.

Perhaps the best way of all to get a horse is to brief an expert to buy one for you. This method of purchase has two big advantages: there is a better-than-average chance of getting a suitable animal; and if the horse turns out to be no good then someone else is to blame.

CARE
AND
MANAGEMENT

This section is intended only as a very general guide to the routine care of a horse or pony, and cannot, of course, be expected to apply to all horses in all situations. Obviously, care of a horse varies with the type of animal it is, the climate in which it lives, the use to which it is being put, and the available local fodder.

Looking after a horse is largely a matter of common sense and hard work. The following general principles of such things as daily inspection, companionship and foot care can be held to apply to any horse or pony, whether in work or not; but the novice horse owner is strongly recommended to apply to his veterinary surgeon for much more specific advice.

Character of the horse

In order to work efficiently with a horse it is necessary to have some understanding of its probable point of view, of what will upset it and what will reassure it, and why this is so. Horses, by and large, are not very intelligent; though the smaller they are, the sharper, so that a very small pony can usually outwit a very small child. Adult-sized mounts, painful as it is to say it, are in general short of brain to the point of stupidity.

In its wild state, from which the domestic horse is barely removed, the dominant instinct is fear. The wild horse survives by suspecting the rock, overhanging tree, ditch, or other cover that can conceal an attacker, and in shying at a fallen log or bolting from an unfamiliar sound, sight or smell the domestic horse is only obeying a wise instinct inherited through millions of years. When threatened, the horse's natural reaction is to run away at top speed, or, when the worst of all possible events comes to pass and it finds something on its back – in the wild state, always an attacker – to buck until the danger is thrown off. Men may feel that the horse exists to carry a rider, but no one ever told the horse about it.

In dealing with fear, and therefore in dealing with all horses, handling should be kind but firm, instructions given clearly and with patience, and sudden movements and sharp voices should be avoided. All horses respond to a gentle, soothing flow of nonsense chat. With a very nervous horse an arm slid quietly over the neck and leaned down heavily on the other side can work wonders because it is reminiscent of the gesture horses use to reassure each other – one head resting over the neck of another.

Herd instinct is another dominant characteristic, so much so that a horse who is a steady riding school hack when out with others will often metamorphose into a disturbing ride when taken out alone. Horses depend very greatly on each other for company and reassurance, and an unfair

The muscles of the horse

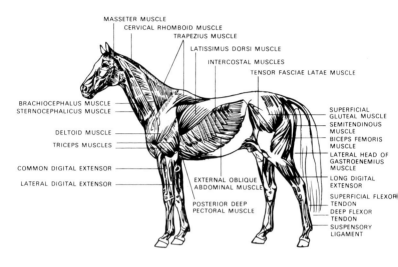

MASSETER MUSCLE
CERVICAL RHOMBOID MUSCLE
TRAPEZIUS MUSCLE
LATISSIMUS DORSI MUSCLE
INTERCOSTAL MUSCLES
TENSOR FASCIAE LATAE MUSCLE

BRACHIOCEPHALUS MUSCLE
STERNOCEPHALICUS MUSCLE

DELTOID MUSCLE

TRICEPS MUSCLES

COMMON DIGITAL EXTENSOR

LATERAL DIGITAL EXTENSOR

SUPERFICIAL
GLUTEAL MUSCLE
SEMITENDINOUS
MUSCLE
BICEPS FEMORIS
MUSCLE
LATERAL HEAD OF
GASTROENEMIUS
MUSCLE
LONG DIGITAL
EXTENSOR
SUPERFICIAL FLEXOR
TENDON
DEEP FLEXOR
TENDON
SUSPENSORY
LIGAMENT

EXTERNAL OBLIQUE
ABDOMINAL MUSCLE

POSTERIOR DEEP
PECTORAL MUSCLE

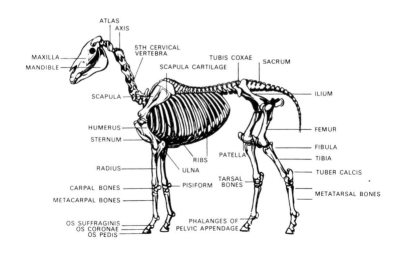

ATLAS
AXIS
5TH CERVICAL
VERTEBRA
TUBIS COXAE
SACRUM

MAXILLA
MANDIBLE

SCAPULA CARTILAGE

ILIUM

SCAPULA

HUMERUS
STERNUM

FEMUR

FIBULA
PATELLA
TIBIA

RADIUS
RIBS
ULNA

TUBER CALCIS

TARSAL
BONES

CARPAL BONES
PISIFORM

METACARPAL BONES

METATARSAL BONES

OS SUFFRAGINIS
OS CORONAE
OS PEDIS

PHALANGES OF
PELVIC APPENDAGE

The skeleton of the horse

strain is put on the animal who is asked to live alone. Failing other horse companionship a donkey will give a lot of comfort, and even a goat or a cow will be better than nothing.

The horse is a creature of habit, appreciating a regular routine and easily upset by unexpected change. Moving homes is traumatic for a horse, and a week or two to settle down and get used to strange surroundings should be allowed to any new purchase before serious work is asked of him. A truly considerate new owner will inquire into the routine practised in the horse's former home, and will make the change to his own routine only gradually. Horses should be fed at the same times every day, caught up from grass with regularity (if brought into the stable daily at, say, 4 o'clock, they will soon learn to wait at the paddock gate at the proper time). If their daily program is too haphazard they may become fractious and difficult to handle.

Horses learn by association. For example, an exercise boy who beat a racehorse filly for running away with him on the gallops handed out the punishment when he was safely back in the stable. The filly continued to run away with him, but soon refused to enter the stable. On a lighter note, though just as valid as an object lesson, I, as a child, trained my pony to follow a ball (I had ambitions to play polo) by throwing apples into his paddock. The pony soon learned to follow the apple. Equipped with an improvised polo stick and an old tennis ball I mounted him, let him catch a glimpse of the now-familiar round shape out of the corner of his eye, and threw the ball. He pursued it with trained accuracy; but when he reached it stopped dead, ate the ball, and I fell off.

Horses, like humans, have widely-differing personalities. Some are bold and relatively outgoing, a few are prima donnas, many are timid and unsure. Nearly all are capable of great affection and some even of loyalty, and the rare "rogue" has usually in his past suffered some injustice from a human. Horses have excellent memories, and loss of temper or bad treatment by a groom or rider will never be forgotten. Deliberate bad behavior should be punished at once, and a single corrective blow with the stick is quite sufficient. Praise for doing well, be it only a single quiet pat down the neck, is always appreciated and is beneficial in training.

The ideal horseman is quiet, kind, unhurried, regular in habit, firm and gentle. If he is unvaryingly so, he has a good chance of becoming the owner of the ideal horse.

Keeping a horse or pony at grass

Horses are wasteful grazers, stripping the best bits of a pasture and leaving the worst to grow rank and rough. Depending on the quality of the grazing, they need at least an acre a head at any one time and can be expected to get through 3 acres a head on a year-round basis (ponies will manage on one acre a head, given good land in a temperate climate). Ideally, three paddocks should be used in turn for 4 or 8 months each on a 1- or 2-year cycle, which allows for the pasture to rest and grow and for a hay crop to be taken off it as food for the following winter. Rotation grazing with cattle or sheep permits the pasture to be evenly cropped and prevents the grass from becoming "horse sick" with worm parasites not harmful to other animals.

Pasture grazed solely by horses soon becomes rank through droppings laid regularly in the same areas, encouraging the growth of nettles and thistles and other unwanted weeds. If rotation grazing with other animals is not practicable, this can be controlled by the daily gathering of the droppings (laborious) or by regular use of a brush harrow to disperse the droppings and by cutting with a gang mower to top the weeds.

The principles of grazing are not yet entirely understood, and it is probable that in the future grazing will be produced that will allow the horse to thrive on a smaller acreage. Anyone who has watched a horse grazing in a varied pasture will know that it grazes selectively, picking dandelions, briar shoots, plantains — all the things that we call "weeds" — to satisfy its palate. This has to do with the different trace elements contained in plants, which are brought to the surface by the varying depth of the roots and the conditions of growth, and is even now imperfectly understood by farmers who plant a mixture of Bennett's grass and clover in the belief that they plant the best. It is as if a conquering Martian, observing only British motorway food, thought that his captives would thrive on an exclusive diet of sausage, egg and chips. "Grazing" does not depend on grass alone, but on a mixture of "weeds" that the horse can select according to its particular need.

Fencing must be sound. If the pasture is surrounded by hedges then they should be stiff enough to stop the horse from walking through. Barbed wire is undesirable because of the damage it can do to an animal; but it is sometimes unavoidable, and in such cases the owner should ensure that it is stretched tight so that the horse's legs cannot become entangled. Gates should swing easily to their gateposts, allowing plenty of passage room for an excited horse, and fastenings should be secure against the most inquisitive and inventive of the breed. Some kind of shelter is needed as a windbreak in foul weather — any three-sided wooden shed will do, provided that the back of it stands against the coldest wind — and shade in summer paddocks can be got from the same shelter, or from a tree or tall hedge. Pastures should be regularly inspected for hazards such as loose wire, broken glass or tin that could cause injury, and hedges should be kept free of poisonous plants such as deadly nightshade and yew.

If there is not a clear stream in the field, fresh water must be provided. A self-filling water tank is the most convenient in cases where the pasture is handy to main drains; otherwise an old tank prevents the need for daily refilling, but needs emptying and scrubbing out at least once a week to keep the water from becoming stale. A constant supply of fresh water is vital to a horse's health. A lump of rock salt left in the field to supplement the inadequate mineral content of most grazing is also desirable.

In the case of native ponies stabling is unnecessary even in the hardest winter. Native ponies are healthier living out all year round, and are not as susceptible to the coughs and colds caused by the drafts and stuffiness endured by stabled animals. But the pony at grass is instinctively greedy, through centuries of having had to scratch a living from poor-quality terrain. In spring and summer, when the rich grass comes up, a pony should be watched very carefully — instinct will tell it to stuff itself while the opportunity lasts, and the result is often laminitis, an inflammation of the spongy membrane inside the hoof. Laminitis is extremely painful — in severe cases the sufferer has to be destroyed — and a grass-fed animal which shows signs of getting too fat must have its food restricted. Stable it during the day (a practice sometimes also necessary to prevent torment from flies) and/or pasture it on poorer grazing.

In winter, the grass-fed horse should be given as much hay as it will eat, even though it does no work. As the grass dies down during the fall and the feed value lessens, start with a quarter of a bale (approximately 14lb) at night and feed more if the animal eats it up. Double the quantity and double the feeding times when snow covers the grass. A haynet is an economy, as horses trample hay fed loose; but the haynet should not be tied too high as hayseeds will fall into the horse's eyes, causing irritation. A hayrack fixed at the height of the horse's head, and installed in its shelter, is ideal

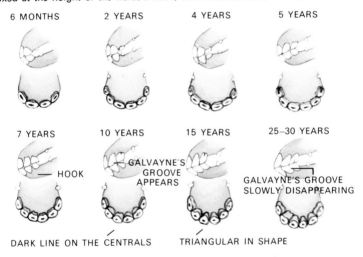

6 MONTHS   2 YEARS   4 YEARS   5 YEARS

7 YEARS   10 YEARS   15 YEARS   25–30 YEARS

— HOOK

GALVAYNE'S GROOVE APPEARS

GALVAYNE'S GROOVE SLOWLY DISAPPEARING

DARK LINE ON THE CENTRALS   TRIANGULAR IN SHAPE

The 6 permanent incisors — centrals, laterals and corners — are the basis for assessing a horse's age. Milk teeth are replaced by permanent teeth by 4½ years of age, and reasonable accuracy can be arrived at up until about 9. At 10, Galvayne's groove appears at the gum of the upper corners, lengthening with age as the teeth angle out. In older horses age is increasingly difficult to tell. Horses over 9 are often loosely described as "aged".

both as a prevention against irritation of the eyes and against the waste of hay through being soaked by rain. If the horse must be fed under the open sky, its favorite place in the field is the best site for economy of fodder.

If the grass-fed horse or pony is in regular work it needs a daily feed or two of nuts or oats mixed with chaff and bran, dampened slightly to bind it and to keep down any possible dust which could get into its lungs. Extra feeding of this kind varies with the amount of work required of the animal and the competence of the rider who will sit on its frisky back. Grated or chopped carrot, root vegetables, or apples mixed into the feed are healthy variations, and horses respond to the consideration of being given extras of this sort.

Animals kept at grass will stay perfectly healthy without grooming — indeed it is essential that the protective grease is left in their coats so that rain and cold and heat do not harm them. It is enough to brush off unsightly mud with a dandy brush and tidy up the mane and tail before exercise. What is most necessary is to pick out the horse's feet each day, both to remove stones picked up in the pasture and also to check the condition of the hooves. Hooves grow about half an inch a month, and regardless of wear shoes should be removed and refitted every four to six weeks to prevent the wall of the hoof from splitting. Unshod horses, even though unused, need regular attendance from the farrier if their feet are to be kept in good health.

Pastured horses should never be turned loose with the sweat still wet on

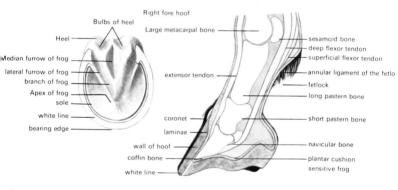

A horse is only as good as its feet. A bruised sole or frog, a stone caught in the lateral cleft of the frog, or bruises or cuts on the bulbs of the heels can and will cause lameness. Care should be taken when riding the horse on stony ground. Excessive wear to the bearing edge in the unshod horse should be avoided as should splitting of the wall of the hoof. Sandcracks — cracks running downwards from the coronet — will cause lameness if deep enough to touch the laminae. Laminitis — inflammation of the laminae — is not uncommon in ponies on rich pasture, and in extreme cases can cause the coffin bone to drop through the wall of the foot. Navicular disease, a corrosive ulcer on the navicular bone, is incurable.

them as they can easily catch a chill. A safe practice at the end of exercise is to walk the last mile home to ensure that the horse is cool and dry before releasing it.

Stabling

Stables can be built of brick, concrete, stone or wood, the last not less than 1in thick and protected with creosote on both sides. Roofing is normally of tile or asbestos sheeting (corrugated iron is undesirable because it is noisy in rain, hot in summer and cold in winter). Looseboxes — stables in which the horse can move freely, as opposed to stalls in which it is tied by the head — are much the most desirable form of accommodation, and the area should be large enough to avoid cramped movements and being "cast" in the box (which happens when a horse lies down so close to a wall that it is unable to do the necessary stretching out of its body to get up). A good size for a loosebox is 10ft by 10ft, with an 8ft clearance at the door rising to a 12ft overhead ridge. If partition walls are used to segregate areas of, for example, a barn, these should be not less than 5ft high to avoid kicking and should have bars above them up to 8ft high to prevent biting. Stable doors facing outwards need overhanging eaves to protect the horse from sunstroke or from the persistent dripping or driving of rain.

Where many horses are kept together, individual looseboxes under one communal roof are popular and practical; either with boxes facing each other across a central aisle, which is advisable in predominantly cold and wet climates and is convenient for labor (though not particularly easy to ventilate), or with boxes facing outwards from a central core which may be used to store fodder.

A rough finish to the flooring is essential to prevent slipping. The floor must be waterproof, either of brick or concrete, and a slight fall of approximately 1:40 is necessary for proper drainage. To avoid flooding and to facilitate drainage the stable floor should be higher than its external surroundings.

Good ventilation is essential to a horse's health, and the lack of it leads to coughs, colds and claustrophobia. Half doors give plenty of fresh air while protecting the body from drafts, and hopper windows permit continued good ventilation when the weather is too bad for the top half of the door to be kept open. Window glass should be set far back in the wall or protected by bars so that the horse cannot break it, and all fastenings, bolts, etc. should be placed out of the horse's reach.

The site of the stable is important, since horses who are bored tend to develop vices such as weaving or windsucking and crib biting, which damage the respiratory system. The view from the stable should provide the occupant with something to look at, at best another horse across the yard or next door to satisfy his herd instinct.

Mangers should be substantial, and placed high enough to stop the horse from getting its front feet in them but not so high as to make eating difficult. Hay racks (more economical than feeding from a pile of loose hay in a corner) should not be higher than the horse's head or it may get hay-seeds in its eyes.

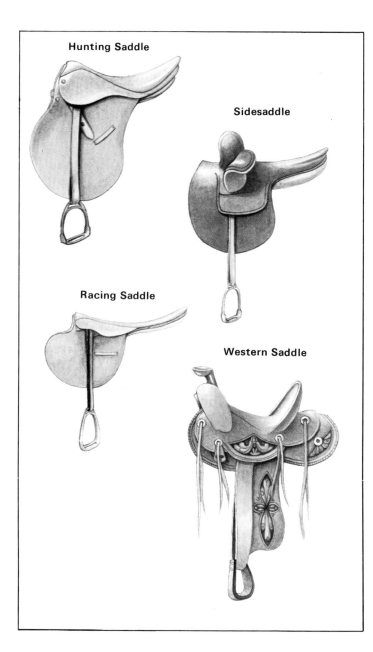

Hunting Saddle

Sidesaddle

Racing Saddle

Western Saddle

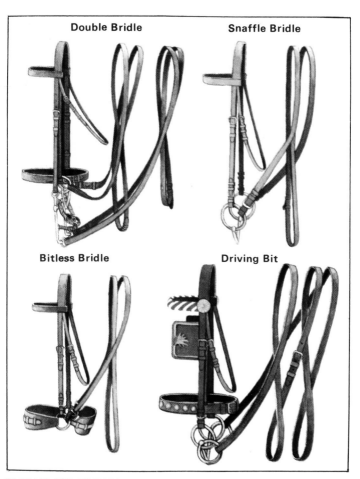

Double Bridle

Snaffle Bridle

Bitless Bridle

Driving Bit

SADDLES AND BRIDLES

Saddles and bridles vary according to the requirements of the rider and the function and strength of the horse. Variations also occur according to differing national fashions.

The double bridle shown is commonly used in cases where an advanced degree of response is needed, as in dressage, or on horses which are too strong to be controlled by the less severe snaffle bit. Bitless bridles, also called hackamores, are popular throughout the Americas. In the hackamore control is effected through pressure on the nose. The racing saddle (opposite) is the lightest saddle made. It has aluminium stirrups, and can weigh as little as 8 oz. In complete contrast, the heavy "armchair-like" Western saddle can support a rider in comfort all day.

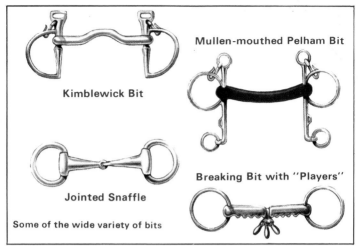

Kimblewick Bit

Mullen-mouthed Pelham Bit

Jointed Snaffle

Breaking Bit with "Players"

Some of the wide variety of bits

Disease

The horse is an extraordinarily delicate animal. It can die from a cough or a belly ache. If it coughs more than twice during the course of exercise, especially if it is a hard, dry cough not followed by a nose-clearing sneeze, it is probably ill and should not be ridden faster than a walk until the cause of the cough has been ascertained. A horse or pony who rolls abnormally much, particularly if accompanied by patchy sweating, is almost certain to be suffering from stomach pain such as colic. Since this can be serious the veterinary surgeon should be sent for at once and the patient kept on the move until he arrives.

A horse is only as good as its legs and feet. Any lameness is a potential disaster. Run a hand down the legs and over the feet each day before exercise, and if any unusual heat is noticeable find out the cause before working the horse.

Grass-fed horses are prone to worms. Unless grazing with cows, which destroy redworm larvae, they should be wormed about three times a year. Tetanus is another hazard, prevalent in many soils and communicable through the smallest scratch or graze. Every horse should have an anti-tetanus injection and two boosters for life immunity (and so should its owner). Stabled horses should also regularly be wormed, most easily done by adding worm powders to the feed.

Listlessness, dull eyes, staring coat, a running nose are all signs of illness, and also there are sores, lumps, scratches, parasites and areas that feel un-naturally hot to be watched for. Daily inspection of the horse and in particular regular handling of its body will soon give an owner a "feel" for his horse's good health and enable him to spot signs of illness at an early stage. Catching a disease before it has had time to develop and sending promptly for the veterinary surgeon is at once humane and in the long run economic.

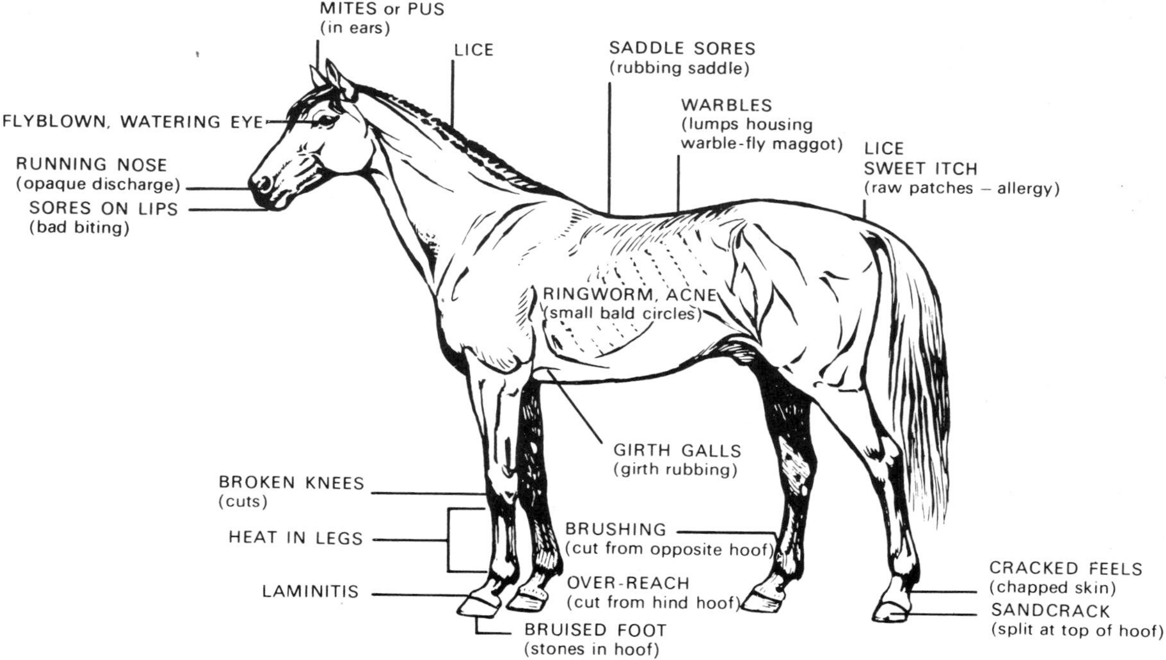

MITES or PUS
(in ears)

FLYBLOWN, WATERING EYE

RUNNING NOSE
(opaque discharge)

SORES ON LIPS
(bad biting)

LICE

SADDLE SORES
(rubbing saddle)

WARBLES
(lumps housing
warble-fly maggot)

LICE

SWEET ITCH
(raw patches – allergy)

CRACKED FEELS
(chapped skin)

SANDCRACK
(split at top of hoof)

RINGWORM, ACNE
(small bald circles)

GIRTH GALLS
(girth rubbing)

BRUSHING
(cut from opposite hoof)

OVER-REACH
(cut from hind hoof)

BRUISED FOOT
(stones in hoof)

BROKEN KNEES
(cuts)

HEAT IN LEGS

LAMINITIS

SEATS OF ILLNESS

Daily routine

If at grass: Visit the horse daily, even in summertime, to check for injury and general condition. Always lift up and pick out the feet, partly to check against broken or worn shoes or hooves and partly to ensure that stones are not lodged in the sensitive parts of the feet. Check the water supply and make periodic checks for damaged fencing and poisonous plants. If the horse is to work the next morning it is often easier to bring him into the stable overnight and dry him off, bed him down and feed him than it is to have to cope with a wet animal the next day when time may be limited.

If stabled: Feeding varies with the size of the animal and the type of work it is required to do, so specific instructions cannot be given here except to say that a varied diet including appetizers such as carrots and apples is far to be preferred to the unvarying feed of horse nuts so often defended by lazy owners, and that a bran mash twice a week to clean the intestines is essential to a horse fed exclusively on hard food. Three feeds a day are far better for a horse's digestion than one enormous meal at night. Fresh hay should be given morning and night — good quality hay is worth a little extra cost, as dust in that of poorer quality will make the animal cough (a far more serious complaint in horses than in humans). Fresh water at all times is essential, and two full buckets of it should be left with the horse overnight.

Bedding should be thoroughly cleaned and replaced each morning, and extra droppings removed at night. The best bed for a horse is clean, deep wheat straw, though greedy horses who eat their straw sometimes need bedding on peat or wood shavings (both of which are difficult to muck out).

Exercise of $1-1\frac{1}{2}$ hours a day is necessary if the horse is kept exclusively in the stable, though most horses benefit from one day of rest each week and on the day following a hard day's hunting a short, quiet walk to ease stiff muscles is usually all that is wanted.

A good grooming every day is essential to the health of a stabled horse. The action of the brush promotes circulation and removes loose hairs which could cause irritation (horses at grass solve these problems by rolling). A horse returning from exercise should never be left in the stable with a wet or damp coat as it could become chilled. A quick way of drying off the body is to heap straw along the wet back and cover with the rug (inverted to prevent the lining from getting damp), while cleaning off the legs with straw. All mud must be removed at this stage — not only is it easier to get it off while it is fresh, but mud that is left to harden later comes away with the many small tearings of the skin which are known as "mud fever". Dry sweat marks should be sponged off with a damp sponge, and mane, tail and coat brushed over before the horse is left for the night — apart from adding greatly to the horse's comfort, this prevents the coat from setting overnight into unwanted waves. Feet, of course, must be cleaned out both before and after exercise, and shoes checked for wear.

Keeping a horse stabled requires 2–3 hours a day of attention, spread over a regular routine from mucking out in the early morning to the last look round at night some 12–15 hours later. Owners who cannot easily afford the time are advised not to attempt to keep a horse in this manner.

COLORS
AND
MARKINGS

COLORS

In terms of color, the word *points* includes mane, tail and most of the legs.

ALBINO: Total lack of pigmentation, resulting in a pure white coat on a pink skin throughout. Eyes pale blue, though dark-eyed albinos have been developed in the United States.

APPALOOSA: Spotted areas on a white ground, or white spots on a dark ground, either partly or all over the horse. Basic coat color usually roan. (See Appaloose, pages 111–5.)

BAY: Brown head and body with black points. Variations according to density of body color are:

   Dark bay – dark brown with black points.

   Light bay – light brown with black points.

   Bright bay – bright reddish-brown with black points.

BAY-BROWN: Color conforming partly, but not exactly, to bay and brown. For example, mane may contain both brown and black hairs.

BLACK: Solid black all over (except where white markings occur on legs or face).

BROWN: All over dark brown, usually nearly black, with brown points of the same density of color.

CALICO: See Pinto.

CHESTNUT: Muted orange body, varying in intensity from reddish to gold, with points of the same color. Chestnuts can be *dark, light* or *bright* according to depth of color. A true chestnut, referred to simply as 'chestnut', is chestnut all over. A variation is *chestnut with blond mane and tail*, distinct from *palomino* because of the deeper coat color.

CREAM: Cream body and points, caused through lack of pigmentation. Skin is pink, eyes light-colored (*wall*) or bluish.

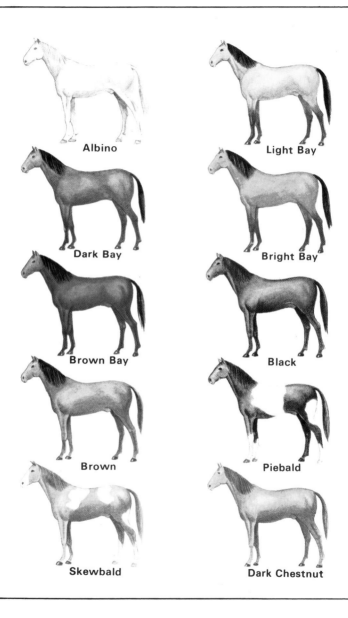

Albino

Light Bay

Dark Bay

Bright Bay

Brown Bay

Black

Brown

Piebald

Skewbald

Dark Chestnut

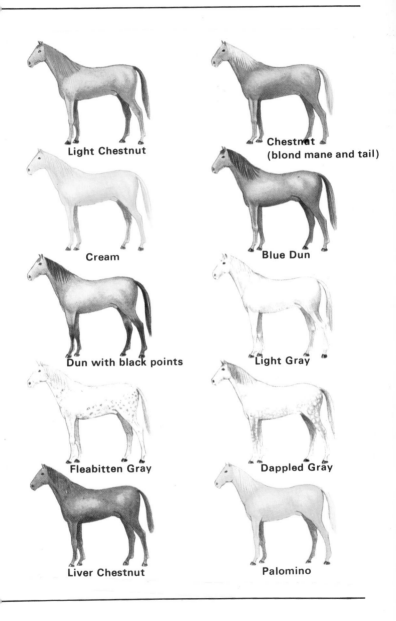

Light Chestnut

Chestnut
(blond mane and tail)

Cream

Blue Dun

Dun with black points

Light Gray

Fleabitten Gray

Dappled Gray

Liver Chestnut

Palomino

DUN: Mouse-colored coat as opposed to brown, sometimes all over but usually with black points (called *dun with black points*). Duns range from *blue dun*, in which a greyish hue prevails, through *mouse* to *golden* or *yellow dun*.

GRAY: A mixture of white and black hairs throughout the coat. Gray horses have black skins except where white markings occur, such as a blaze or stocking, under which the skin is pink. They are born near-black or dark (*iron*) gray and become whiter with age. A horse with a mainly white coat on a black skin is called a *light gray* (as opposed to a pure white *albino*). *Fleabitten gray* occurs when the dark hairs are present in tufts. *Dappled gray*, usually more evident in summer or clipped coats, shows dark circles on a lighter ground.

LIVER CHESTNUT: Subdued chestnut, closer to dun or brown than a true chestnut.

ODD-COLORED: Conforming to no fixed color.

PAINT: See Pinto.

PALOMINO: Creamy-golden body with flaxen mane and tail.

PIEBALD: Body marked in large, irregular patches of white and black.

PINTO: North American word embracing *piebald* and *skewbald*; synonymous with *paint* and *calico*.

SKEWBALD: Body marked in large, irregular patches of white and any other color except black.

SORREL: American name for *chestnut*.

MARKINGS

BLAZE: A broad white mark down the face.

SNIP: A white mark between the nostrils.

STAR: A white mark on the forehead.

STRIPE: A thin white mark running down the face.

WHITE FACE: A blaze wide enough to cover forehead and eyes, extending over nose and most or all of the muzzle.

SOCK: White leg extending upwards from the hoof over the fetlock joint.

STOCKING: White leg extending upwards from the hoof to the knee or hock.

WHITE CORONET, WHITE PASTERN, ETC.: A small amount of white covering only the part named.

DORSAL STRIPE/DONKEY STRIPE: Black or dark brown line running along the spine.

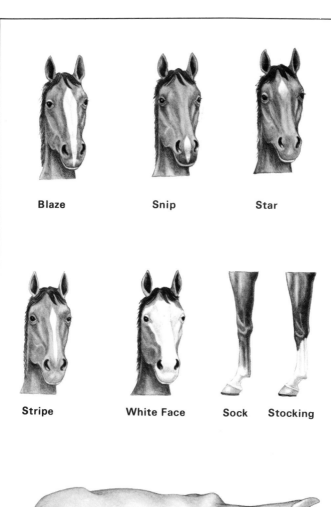

Blaze **Snip** **Star**

Stripe **White Face** **Sock** **Stocking**

Dorsal Stripe/Donkey Stripe

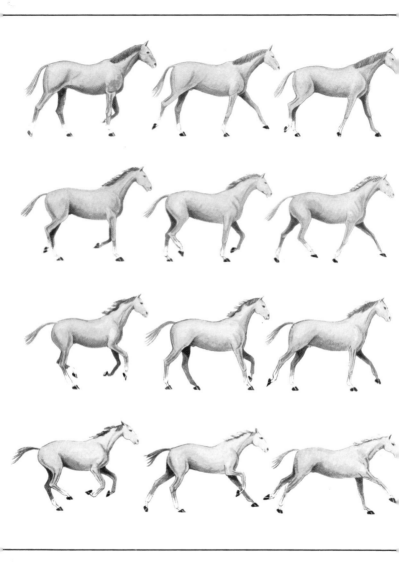

THE FOUR NATURAL GAITS OF THE HORSE

The horse's gait varies according to the speed at which it moves. The walk, the slowest gait, is a 4-beat gain in which each foot comes down separately. In the trot, a 2-beat gait, the opposing fore and hind feet hit the ground

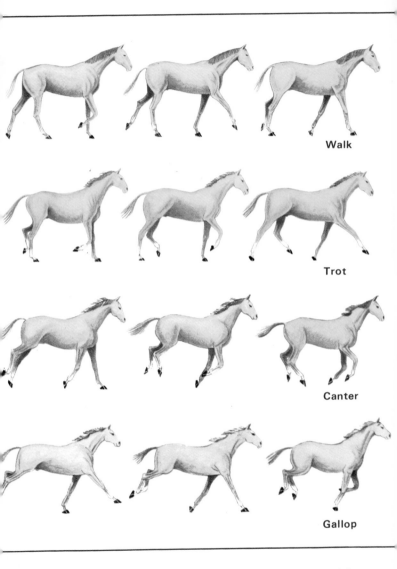

Walk

Trot

Canter

Gallop

simultaneously. The canter, which to a casual eye may seem a slowed-down version of the gallop, is in fact a 3-beat gait; whereas the gallop, at which the horse is fully extended, is a 4-beat gait wherein each foot can be heard to strike the ground separately.

GLOSSARY

ACTION: Descriptive of the movement of the legs at all paces.

BARREL: The ribcage area of the body, roughly from girth to hip.

BOTH LEGS COMING OUT OF ONE HOLE: Front legs which are set too closely together at the top.

COLDBLOOD: Heavy, bovine sort of horse suitable for farm work by strength and calm temperament. Very probably descended from Northern Forest type (see WARMBLOOD).

COLT: An entire male horse under 4 years old.

CONFORMATION: Word describing the build of a horse as a whole.

COW-HOCKED: When the hocks, viewed from behind, angle in towards each other, as in a cow.

CRIB BITING: Vice developed through boredom. Horse grasps manger, top of stable door or fencing in its teeth and swallows air.

DEEP THROUGH THE GIRTH: Good depth from just behind the withers to just behind the elbow, allowing plenty of heart and lung room.

ENTIRE: Synonymous with STALLION – an uncastrated male horse capable of being used at stud.

EWE NECK: Describes a concave line of neck from ears to withers. A fault of conformation.

FEATHER: Long hair on the legs, springing from the back of the fetlock and sometimes continuing up the back of the leg almost to the knee.

FILLY: Female horse under 4 years old.

FLAT-SIDED: Descriptive of a flat ribcage that is not rounded or WELL SPRUNG. Tends to restrict expansion of lungs.

FOAL: Horse under 1 year old, as COLT FOAL, FILLY FOAL.

FOREHAND: The front part of a horse, comprising head, neck, shoulders and forelegs.

GELDING: Castrated male horse.

GOOSE-RUMPED: Rump inclines sharply downwards from point of hip to tail. A fault of conformation.

HAND: Term of measurement for a horse. 1 hand = 4in. The height is taken from the highest point of the withers to the ground. A horse is described as being so many hands high, which is usually abbreviated in print as hh.

HINNY: Offspring of a horse or pony stallion and a female donkey.

HOCKS WELL LET DOWN: Hocks set low on long gaskins, resulting in short cannon bones. A most desirable point of conformation.

LIGHT-FRAMED: Having a slender bone structure, which gives an unsubstantial appearance.

MARE: Female horse aged 4 or more years.

MULE: Offspring of a donkey stallion and a horse or pony mare.

PIGGY EYE: Abnormally small eye. A fault of conformation.

PIN- or PIGEON-TOED: The feet point in towards each other. A fault of conformation.

PLENTY OF BONE: Usually chiefly (though not necessarily) applied to the legs, descriptive of good density of bone. A desirable quality.

PONY: Equine standing not more than 14.2hh (158in tall) at the withers, regardless of type. From 14.2$\frac{1}{2}$hh (158$\frac{1}{2}$in) up, it is called a horse.

ROACH-BACKED: Prominent convex protusion of the spine in the area of the loins, caused by malformation of the spinal column.

SICKLE HOCKS: Hocks which, when seen from the side, are bent too strongly at the joint, making the line from hock to ground angled forwards instead of vertical. A structural weakness.

SPLAYED FEET: The hooves point outwards away from each other. A fault of conformation.

STALLION: An entire male horse aged 4 or more years.

TIED-IN BELOW THE KNEE: Where the bone immediately below the knee is narrower than the bone halfway down the cannon bone. A serious weakness.

UPRIGHT PASTERN: The angle of the pastern between the fetlock joint and the hoof inclines too closely to the vertical. A bad fault, as it causes the pasterns to jar easily on roads or other hard ground.

UPRIGHT SHOULDER: Where the angle from the point of the shoulder to the withers inclines more to the vertical than is desirable. A fault which inhibits free movement of the front legs, usually resulting in a short, scrappy action.

WARMBLOOD: Fine-boned type of horse, usually suitable for riding, as opposed to the more solid and more even-tempered COLDBLOOD. In some countries, distinguished as horses containing a strain of Arab blood. The fine overlap between "warmblood" and "coldblood" is still largely a matter of personal opinion.

WEAVING: Vice developed through boredom, often in imitation of another horse. Horse rocks from side to side. This prevents it from resting properly, and so limits the work it can do.

WELL-RIBBED-UP: Describes a horse with good heart and lung room under the ribcage. The front ribs are set relatively flat, with the back or floating ribs "sprung" or rounded, providing plenty of room inside.

WELL SET/WELL SET ON: Commendatory terms describing a favorable angle of meeting between one part of the body and another; for example, neck well set on shoulder.

WELL-SPRUNG RIBS: Term of commendation describing floating ribs which are hooped outwards, giving ample interior room. (See WELL-RIBBED-UP.)

WELL-TOPPED: Denotes good conformation above the legs.

BREED GUIDE

PONIES

FALABELLA

Origin: Argentina.
Height: Under 7hh.
Color: All colors.
Character: Friendly and intelligent, ideal as a pet.

The Falabella is the smallest horse in the world. It takes its name from the Falabella family, who developed it on their Recreo de Roca Ranch near Buenos Aires. The breed is descended from a small Thoroughbred owned by the family, and has been inbred to the smallest Shetlands; but, though the Falabella is less than a century old, no records of its early development exist and its precise origins will never be known.

It is a hardy miniature horse, full of character, and is popular in North America as a harness pony and as a pet. Extreme downgrading in size has caused it to lose much of its physical strength, and it cannot be regarded as a serious riding pony.

Any color is acceptable in the breed, though modern breeders are tending to concentrate on Appaloosa markings.

SHETLAND

Origin. Northern Scotland – Shetland and Orkney Islands.
Height: Average 9.3hh, should not exceed 10.2. Smallest recorded specimen 6.2hh (26in).
Color: Any, including piebald, skewbald and dun. Black and dark brown are the most common.
Character: Very gentle disposition, with great courage and character.

Falabella

Easy to train, sure-footed and adaptable, it makes an ideal first pony for a child and is also excellent for driving and light carting.

Physique: For its size considered the strongest of all breeds, capable of pulling twice its own weight (twice the power of most heavy horses). Head small and sometimes with a concave face. Eyes large and kindly, ears small, muzzle small with open nostrils. Abundant mane, with thick tail often long enough to sweep the ground. Very heavy winter coat, summer coat fine and sleek. Back short, strong, and deep through the girth. Legs very hard, with short cannon bones and small feet, and straight, light action.

The Shetland is an ancient breed. The earliest remains found in the Shetland Islands are dated about 500 BC, when the pony was apparently domesticated. The breed has remained unchanged apart from some cross-breeding with the now-extinct, small, black Lofoten pony of Norway, which was brought to the Shetlands by Norse settlers about 1,000 years ago and was also adapted to island life. It is extremely hardy, having bred for millenia in a cold, exposed land with no trees and very little shelter. It is used by the Shetland islanders for all working purposes, and in the mid-19th century was much in demand as a pit pony to work in the coalmines of northern England.

The Shetland's strength is legendary. A nine-hand Shetland is recorded (1820) as having carried a 170-lb man 40 miles in one day. The Reverend John Brand, writing in 1701, was also impressed with the Shetland's strength:

Some not so high as others prove to be the strongest, yea there are some, whom an able man can lift up in his arms, yet will they carry him and a woman behind him eight miles forward and as many back.

Theories about the origins of the Shetland conflict, one authority claiming that it came down from the Tundra during the Ice Age, crossing the frozen Norwegian Sea before the retreat of the ice fields from the British Isles; that the island isolation and inbreeding of the following millenia caused the pony's size to be reduced from an original height of around 13.2hh. Another theory is based on recognizable "Shetlands" which appear in Old Stone Age paintings in the caves of the Dordogne and Altamira. It proposes that Shetlands may have been the first equines brought to Britain by human agency, since one of the earliest waves of human immigrants came to Britain from the Biscay area, and suggests that Shetlands were probably a dwarf variety, split off from the main body of ponies of Exmoor type. This second theory seems the more acceptable, since ponies would have had a hard time of it on the Tundra during the Ice Age and it seems more probable that a northward rather than a southward move into the tough conditions of the Shetland Islands would have stunted the ponies' size.

AMERICAN SHETLAND

Origin: United States.
Height: Up to 11.2hh.
Color: All colors.
Character: Highly intelligent, gentle and adaptable.
Physique: Taller and lighter in build than its Island ancestor; head more refined, often with a faint inward dish, ears dainty. High, exaggerated action reminiscent of a miniature Hackney, often with artificially-developed gaits. Despite its seeming delicacy, still strong enough to pull twice its own weight.

The American Shetland was developed in the USA by selective breeding from quality imports of the original Island type, which is stockier than the American version. It is popular throughout northern America, and demand has sent its value to heights that would be more realistic for a Thoroughbred racehorse. As early as 1957 an American Shetland stallion fetched $85,000 at auction, and another has since been syndicated for $90,000. (NB Ponies not especially suitable for breeding still command only pony prices.)

The breed's adaptability is shown by the many uses to which it is put. In addition to their primary functions as children's ponies and general household pets, Shetlands appear in the show ring in both halter and harness classes (sometimes the ponies' tail muscles are nicked to give an artificially high carriage and false tails are added, and sometimes false hooves are fitted to make their feet seem longer); on the racetrack, trotting before tiny, lightweight racing sulkies (Shetlands have clocked 1.55 on a half-mile track); and in Pulling Contests, where the ponies compete to pull a percentage of their own weight.

Shetland

American Shetland

GREEK PONIES

SKYROS: Greece's smallest pony, the Skyros, stands 9.1–11hh. It comes from the island of Skyros, where it is used as a pack pony and for light agricultural work. On the mainland it is more commonly used as a riding pony for young children. It is a finely-built breed of great antiquity, often cow-hocked and with upright shoulders, and its most common colors are dun, brown and gray.

PINDOS: Pindos ponies, bred in the mountains and foothills of Thessaly and Epirus, stand 12–13hh and are used for riding and light agricultural tasks. They are strong, hardy mountain ponies, light in build and of Oriental origin. They are often gray, or may be dark in color. Pindos mares are frequently used to breed mules.

PENEIA: Peneia, in the Peloponnese, has its own breed of pony which is used for farm work and as a pack pony. It is of Oriental type, a lightweight pony which does well on poor fare, is a willing worker, and is extremely hardy. Peneia ponies range from 10–14hh and come in most colors, brown, bay, chestnut and gray being the most common. The stallions are often used for breeding hinnies.

LANDAIS

Origin: France – Landes.
Height: About 12hh or a little less.
Color: Gray.
Physique: Slight-framed and light of bone, small, expressive head, straight neck, sloping croup. Long mane and tail.

The Landais pony, or *Poney Landais*, is semi-wild and lives in the forests of the Landes. It is closely related to the larger (because more richly-fed) pony of the plains of the Chalosse near the Adour river, and to the Barthais pony, which lives in the marshes of this river. Both these types are usually chestnut or black.

While on the subject of French ponies, mention should be made of the tiny Pottok, a native of the Basque region. It is similar to the Shetland in appearance, though lighter in build, comes in many colors including piebald and skewbald, and is completely wild.

GARRANO (MINHO)

Origin: Portugal – Garrano do Minho and Traz dos Montes.
Height: 10–12hh.
Color: Usually dark chestnut.
Physique: Light-framed pony of excellent conformation. Abundant mane and tail. Strong, surefooted, and extremely hardy.

Skyros

Peneia

The Garrano, also known as the Minho, is by far the commonest pony breed in Portugal. Bred in the rich mountain pastures of the provinces Garrano do Minho and Traz dos Montes, and sometimes carrying Arab blood in its pedigree, it is a pony of great quality and is much in demand for riding and for pack work. It is an historic breed which has survived relatively unchanged for thousands of years. Palaeolithic cave paintings of the Garrano still exist; much later is it said to have provided one of the many foundation blood lines of the Andalusian horse.

Quality Garranos are a speciality of the famous horse fairs at Vila Real and Famalicao, where in the past they competed in traditional races run at a collected trot.

CASPIAN

Origin: Persia — Elburtz Mountains, Caspian Sea.
Height: 10–12hh.
Color: Gray, brown, bay, chestnut.
Character: Gentle, tractable and quick-witted. Ideal mount for a small child in rough country.
Physique: In type more like a miniature horse than a pony. Arab-type head, with small ears and large, prominent eyes. Fine bone, short back, and tail set high and carried gaily. Mane and tail fine and silky. Sure-footed, quick on its feet, and has remarkable jumping ability.

The Caspian is thought, though not proven, to be the native wild horse of Iran which was used by the Mesopotamians in the third millenium BC and coveted by the Achaemenians and Sassanians for ceremonial purposes from the 5th century BC to the 7th century AD. For more than 1,000 years thereafter this animal was believed to be extinct, until in the spring of 1965 a few Caspians were found pulling carts in the coastal towns on the Caspian Sea and grazing along the shoreline. Comparative bone and blood studies have been carried out and the great similarity of size, head structure, and slimness of bone has made researchers optimistic about tracing a connection between the Caspian of today and the ancient miniature horse of Mesopotamia.

Although bones of wild horses have been found in Mesolithic cave remains near Kermanshah in ancient Media, the area described by Greek writers as the homeland of the small horse, no miniature horses are to be found there now. Records suggest that some time during the last thousand years tribes from Kermanshah were exiled to Kalar Dasht on the northern slopes of the Elburtz Mountains, and that these tribes took ponies with them.

DULMEN

Origin: West Germany — Westphalia.
Height: About 12.3hh.
Color: All colors. Black, brown and dun are the most common.

Caspian

Dulmen

The Dülmen is one of the two native pony breeds of Germany. The other is the almost-extinct (or possibly completely extinct – authorities differ) Senner pony, which is (or was) extremely tough and which runs (or ran) wild in the forests of the Teutoberger Wald. Both these ponies contributed to the ancestry of the Hanoverian horse.

The Dülmen pony is also a vanishing breed. The main herd of a hundred mares runs semi-wild in a reserve on the Meerfelder Bruch in Westphalia, where they are said to have been bred for more than six centuries. They are the property of the Duke of Cröy, and are no longer purebred through having been outcrossed to imported Polish and British pony stallions. Each year the Dülmen herd is rounded up and the yearling colts and other unwanted stock are caught and sold.

GOTLAND

Origin: Sweden – Gotland Island.
Height: 12–12.2hh.
Color: Dun, black, brown, bay, chestnut, gray, palomino.
Character: Gentle and easy to handle, though inclined to be obstinate.
Physique: Lightweight pony with small, straight head, small ears, and short, muscular neck. Strong shoulders; rather long back; tail low-set on sloping quarters. Legs hard and strong, though light of bone, and feet small and hard. Moves well at a walk and trot, gallops badly, and is an outstanding jumper.

Gotland

The Gotland is a prehistoric breed and is thought to be one of the direct descendants of the Tarpan. Certainly it shares many characteristics with such as the Konik, the Huçul, and the now-extinct Lofoten pony. It is believed to be the oldest Scandinavian breed, and is relatively pure-bred except for some infusions of Oriental blood about a century ago. Records indicate that it has run wild on Gotland Island, in the Baltic Sea to the southeast of Sweden, since the Stone Age, and there is still a herd of Gotlands in the forest at Löjsta. It is now also bred on the Swedish mainland.

Formerly in demand for light agricultural work, it is now popular as a children's pony, as a jumper, and for trotting races, for which it is specially bred. It is also called the Skogsruss pony.

ICELAND

Origin: Iceland.
Height: 12–13hh; occasionally bigger.
Color: Usually gray or dun. Also dark brown, chestnut, cream, palomino, and occasionally black, piebald, skewbald.
Character: Docile, friendly; though, like all small pony breeds, it is very independent. It has a remarkable homing instinct, and can be ridden for great distances by a borrower in the sure knowledge that when it is turned loose it will directly find its way home. It responds better to the voice than to the usual aids of horsemanship, and is mostly controlled by the voice alone.
Physique: One of the toughest of all breeds, extremely hardy and rugged. Large head, intelligent eye. Short, thick neck on a short, stocky body; strong, clean legs, hard feet. Abundant mane and tail. It possesses exceptionally good eyesight. Riding ponies are taught an ambling gait, popular in medieval times but now a rarity except in the Americas.

Iceland was first settled in 871 AD by Norwegians who were at odds with Harold Fairhair, who had proclaimed himself king of all Norway the year before and was not unanimously popular. Until that time no larger animal than the Arctic Fox was to be found in Iceland, but the Norwegian immigrants brought ponies and other domestic livestock with them, and subsequently ponies from Norse colonies in Scotland, its islands, Ireland and the Isle of Man were introduced with new settlers. These hardy, homogenous Northern pony types interbred to become the Iceland pony, though four separate types are still just about recognizable to the connoisseur. One of these, the Faxafloi, bred in the south-west of Iceland, looks quite like the Exmoor pony.

An Icelandic speciality, possibly connected with the Norwegian cult of Frey but much more probably arising out of a need for excitement and the lack of game animals to satisfy a basic bloodthirstiness, was horsefighting. The sagas are full of it; "Starkad had a good horse of chestnut hue and it was thought that no horse was his match in fight" starts off the story of the battle of that horse and Gunnar's brown described in the *Saga of Burnt Njal*, which began as a blood feud and ended in a massacre. Owners were expected to go into the ring to assist their stallions during these fights, and were not allowed to touch their opponent's horse (though they were just as likely to be savaged as their horse was).

Since Iceland until recently had no roads and very few tracks smooth enough for the passage of wheels, the value of the Iceland pony for pack and communications purposes was inestimable. This was heightened on one-way journeys by the pony's ability to go home by itself. Up until this century the ponies were also exported to the British Isles to work in the coalmines and as pack and draught animals, and, in the teeth of strong competition from the good native British breeds, were much in demand for their strength, endurance, and good nature.

Modern attempts to refine the Iceland pony with Thoroughbred blood have failed, since the offspring appear to inherit the good qualities of neither parent. Today's Iceland pony divides loosely into pack, riding, and draught types, with an emphasis on the first two, though all are fit to ride if the occasion warrants it. Since beef cattle cannot endure the hard Icelandic winters ponies are also used for food, separate herds being kept for meat and for work.

EXMOOR

Origin: England — Devon and Somerset.
Height: 11.2–12.3hh.
Color: Bay, brown, mouse dun. All have "mealy" (cream-colored) muzzle and a tendency to mealy underbelly and inside thighs. No white markings of any kind.
Character: Intelligent and naturally wild. Once broken they are alert, kindly and excellent companions. They make splendid children's ponies provided they are properly handled early on.
Physique: Elegant head with wide nostrils, broad forehead, and prominent eyes (known locally as "frog" or "toad" eyes). Ears short, thick, and pointed. Neck short and thick, set on a deep, broad chest with shoulder well back. Medium-length back with powerful loins, strong quarters, clean, hard legs and small, hard feet. It has a free, straight action, and has great powers of endurance. The coat is of a peculiar texture, being hard and springy: in summer it lies close and shines like brass; in winter it carries no bloom.

Exmoors are the oldest of the British native breeds, and since ponies are not indigenous to Britain it must be assumed that it walked there before the country became an island. It was known in prehistoric times, and may have been the "Celtic" pony used to pull the war chariots of the Celts (if not, it was a very close relation). It inhabits the wild expanse of open moorland called Exmoor which lies partly in Devon and partly in Somerset, both counties in the south-west of England, and is hardy enough to survive winters which sometimes bring several feet of snow without shelter and without extra food from man.

Iceland

Exmoor

These little animals are tough, and have exceptional guts and spring. Writing in 1820, one William Youatt says,

The Exmoor ponies, although generally ugly enough [his opinion only], are hardy and useful. A well-known sportsman says, that he rode one of them half-a-dozen miles, and never felt such power and action in so small a compass before. To show his accomplishments, he was turned over a gate at least eight inches higher than his back; and his owner, who rides fourteen stone [196 lbs], travelled on him from Bristol to South Moulton, eighty-six miles, beating the coach which runs the same road.

The Reverend John Russell, of roughly the same period, believed that no hunter was of any use without a strain of Exmoor blood. He preferred his horses to be three-parts Thoroughbred to one part Exmoor.

In general, outcrosses with Exmoors to produce a bigger local type did not endure, being at the least unable to survive the rough natural conditions of their pony ancestors. Today the maximum permitted height for stallions is 12.3hh; that for mares is 12.2.

DARTMOOR

Origin: England — Devon.
Height: Up to 12.2hh.
Color: Bay, black and brown are preferred. Odd colors such as piebald and skewbald exist, but they are not recognized by the breed society. Excessive white is discouraged.
Character: Kind and sensible. Ideal first ponies.
Physique: Small, aristocratic head with very small, pricked ears. Strong, sloping shoulders; strong, well-muscled back, loins and quarters. Slim, hard legs and tough, well-shaped feet. Tail high-set and plentiful; abundant mane. Good action, low and free as befits a riding pony. Surefooted and given to longevity.

The Dartmoor is a near relation of the Exmoor, being bred on the neighbouring Devon moor and subject to the same exposed climatic conditions. William Youatt (see Exmoor) also had his opinions on this breed:

There is on Dartmoor a breed of ponies much in request in that vicinity, being sure-footed and hardy, and admirably calculated to scramble over the rough roads and dreary wilds of that mountainous district. The Dartmoor pony is larger than the Exmoor [maybe it was], and, if possible, uglier. He exists there almost in a state of nature. The late Captain Colgrave, governor of the prison, had a great desire to possess one of them of somewhat superior figure to its fellows; and having several men to assist him, they separated it from the herd. They drove it on some rocks by the side of a tor. A man followed on horseback, while the captain stood below watching the chase. The little animal, being driven into a corner, leaped completely over man and horse and escaped.

Dartmoor

From long beyond the memory of man ponies of a small, hardy riding type have lived on Dartmoor, but until the end of the last century they were not registered and they varied much in type. A Dartmoor section of the Polo Pony Society's (now the National Pony Society) stud book was begun in 1899, and the standard has remained without much alteration ever since. The breed was hard-hit in World War II because Dartmoor was used as a training centre for the army, and when the war was finished only ponies passed by inspection or placed at chosen shows were allowed into the stud book. In 1957 the stud book was closed to all except the offspring of registered ponies, and in 1961 a stringent up-grading register was begun. SR1, the first grade, was closed in 1966 with 280 entries; but SR2, the second grade, is open indefinitely. SR1 ponies are branded with the Dartmoor Pony Society's triangle on the neck.

If all this may sound over-particular, it is the result of a peculiar problem which has confronted breeders of the Dartmoor pony in its natural habitat. Less than a hundred years ago, when the demand for very small ponies to work in coalmines was at its peak, Shetland stallions were introduced to Dartmoor to run wild and breed with the native ponies, and the resulting degeneration of the breed was widespread. It is a credit to the Dartmoor Pony Society and to the few individual breeders outside Dartmoor that this perfect child's first pony survives in its purebred form.

WELSH MOUNTAIN PONY (SECTION A)

Origin: Wales.
Height: Not over 12hh (usually not much smaller).
Color: Any color except piebald and skewbald. Gray, brown and chestnut are the most common.
Character: High-spirited pony with great intelligence, courage and endurance.
Physique: Small, Arab-type head, gaily carried, with open nostrils, slightly concave face, bold eye, and small, pointed ears. Graceful neck well-set on deep, sloping shoulders. Short, muscular back on a deep girth and well-sprung ribs. Hindquarters lengthy and fine. Tail set high (another resemblance to the Arab) and carried gaily. Legs fine and hard, short in the cannon bone; the humerus is upright, so that the foreleg is not set in under the body. Feet small, round and hard. The action, typical of a pony reared on mountainous terrain, is quick and free in all paces, moving well away in front, and with the hocks well flexed and under the body to give powerful leverage.

This small, aristocratic-looking riding pony is considered by many to be the most beautiful of all the British mountain and moorland breeds. It is popular all over Britain, Europe and North America and is extensively bred outside its native country, though breeders often import fresh blood from Wales to keep their stock true to its native type.

Historical references to Welsh ponies go back surprisingly far. The *Welsh Stud Book* refers to the Romans crossing Arabs with the mountain ponies; which is wrong, but is entirely excusable not only because of the Arab-like appearance of the pony but because the historical documents from which they got their information are misleading. Records of breeding the Welsh pony (or it would be fairer to say of pony-breeding in Wales) go back to Julius Caesar, who appears to have founded a stud at Lake Bala, Merioneddshire, and who introduced some Oriental blood. Here is the source of the confusion, as translators of the original documents tended to interpret a horse of Oriental breed as being "Arab", whereas in Roman times the Arab was not a breed as such and "Arab" was not one of the 12 breeds mentioned by the Romans.

Arabs did have a hand in it, but not until much later. Within the last two or three centuries at least two Arab stallions have run wild on the Welsh hills, breeding freely with the native ponies, and it is no doubt to them that the modern Welsh Mountain pony owes its Arab look. Cob, Hackney, and even Andalusian blood is believed also to have contributed, albeit several centuries ago.

Herds of ponies still live wild on the mountains and moorlands of Wales on the principle of survival of the fittest, and so hardiness and resistance to disease remain inbred. Annual roundups for branding and for weeding out unwanted stock or selected stock for sale have attracted buyers from all over Europe in recent times, and Welsh pony breeding has become a

Welsh Mountain Pony

profitable business. In the light of modern prices it is strange to remember that as recently as 1948 a pony could be bought unbroken off the moors for as little as twelve shillings and sixpence (approx. $1.50).

The Welsh Mountain pony (Section A in the *Welsh Stud Book*) is the foundation stock for Sections B, C and D. It is also a prime contributor to most of Britain's hunting and show ponies, and is predominant in many ponies under 13.2hh.

AMERICAN WELSH PONY

Height: American Stud Book, Section A: not exceeding 12.2hh. Ponies standing 12.3–14hh are listed as Section B in both American and British stud books.
Color: All colors except pinto.
Character and Physique: See Welsh Mountain pony.

In the United States and Canada the name *Welsh pony* covers those ponies that the British separate into Welsh Mountain and Welsh; and since distinctions are made on the basis of height rather than of type this is fair enough. But it is the diminutive Welsh Mountain pony which originally captivated American breeders, and which continues to do so today. Infusions of native blood from studs in Wales have helped to keep the American version pure and true to type, though it is more than anything due to the genuine enthusiasm that this breed evokes and the tact and good sense of the American breed society that the American Welsh pony has not degenerated into a pampered neurotic.

Welsh ponies are used for riding, for show, and as harness ponies. They make marvelous children's ponies, and for bravery, for lightness of heart and for companionability are very hard to equal.

WELSH PONY (SECTION B)

Origin: Wales.
Height: 12–13.2hh.
Color, Character, Physique: Same as for Section A, but particular emphasis is laid on the suitability of this pony as a quality riding pony for children, both in looks, action, and kind temperament.

The Welsh pony is a taller version of the Welsh Mountain pony. It owes a genealogical debt to a small Thoroughbred stallion called Merlin, a direct descendant of the Darley Arabian (see Thoroughbred), who ran wild on the Denbighshire hills at the end of the 18th or beginning of the 19th century. Section B ponies are called "Merlins" to this day.

WELSH PONY (SECTION C)

Origin: Wales.
Height: Not to exceed 13.2hh.
Color, Character, Physique: Those of a scaled-down Welsh cob, smaller and lighter in build. It is a hardy, active pony, stout-hearted, willing and a good doer on poor fare.

The Section C pony, or Welsh Pony of Cob Type, was formerly most in demand as a harness pony and might have declined in numbers through inadequate competition with the motor vehicle. Fortunately, trekking holidays have saved it from becoming a museum piece for the connoisseur. Its strong build gives it enough substance for adults to sit on without guilt, and its kind temperament and ability to thrive on heavy work make it a perfect mount for the increasing numbers of holiday-makers who flock to Wales for a taste of the outdoor life.

In summing up the Welsh breeds which stem from the Mountain pony, the original *Welsh Stud Book* of 1902 says quite simply why these animals are special:

There are several distinct types of these Ponies and Cobs: the small hardy original Mountain type, those somewhat larger bred on lower grounds, those more of the Cob type and lastly the larger Cob. Although quite distinct in appearance and height, still they have the same family likeness, true pony character, air and action, which latter is remarkable for its freedom and dash.

Welsh Pony (Section B)

WELSH COB (SECTION D)

Origin: Wales.
Height: Usually 14–15.1 hh.
Color: Any color except piebald and skewbald. Bay, black, brown, chestnut and roan are most commonly found.
Character: Bold and energetic, an intelligent animal with an equable temperament and a pony character.
Physique: The build resembles a heavier, scaled-up Welsh Mountain pony. Head small and full of quality; eyes bold and wide-set, ears small and pricked. Neck long and proudly-carried, setting into strong shoulders; forelegs set square and forward, not tied in at the elbow. Body strong, deep-girthed and muscular, hindquarters lengthy and powerful, tail high-set and proud. Legs strong with plenty of bone below the knee and a little silky feather on the fetlocks (coarse, wiry hair is objected to). Feet well-shaped and dense, the action free, straight and forceful. At a trot the knee should be bent and the whole foreleg extended straight from the shoulder and as far forward as possible; hocks flexed under the body in straight, powerful leverage. An animal of great stamina, surefooted, strong and brave. A natural jumper, also famous for speed and soundness.

As can be seen from its resemblance to the prepotent Welsh Mountain pony, the Welsh cob evolved on its own home ground. The mixture of foreign blood that gave it its height and strength can only be guessed at – and loosely guessed at that – but in 1188 the Archdeacon of Brecon, one Gerald de Barri, while travelling in a mid-Welsh district called Powys, came across

most excellent studs put apart for breeding, and deriving their origin from some fine Spanish horses, which Robert de Belesme, Count of Shrewsbury, brought into this country; on which account the horses sent from hence are remarkable for their majestic proportion and astonishing fleetness.

In their excellent book *The Foals Of Epona*, writers Anthony Dent and Daphne Machin Goodall say that these 11th-century Spanish horses were

just the kind of animal that a Norman baron would consider worth importing even at considerable expense. They were the ancestors of the famous Andalusian breed, which in turn was the ancestor of the modern Lipizzaner, by way of the Neapolitan; but they also managed, by their union with Welsh mountain mares, to engender the Welsh cob, which under the name of "Powis horse" was to provide so many remounts for English armies from the 13th century onwards. Astonishing fleetness and majestic proportions are of course both relative; the former by contrast with the lumbering Norman destrier, and the latter by contrast with the Welsh pony. But then, under-statement was never one of Gerald's literary faults.

At what point the Powys cob merged into the Welsh cob, and what variations took place in the centuries between (it is suggested here and there that the Welsh cob may have been blood-brother to the now-extinct Welsh carthorse), it is beyond my ability to guess; but the Welsh cob of today and the Powys cob of 800 years ago were very much alike to look at. Assuming equal ability, the medieval horseman was in the happy position of possessing, at a time when horse breeds were not all that versatile, an animal that could carry him into battle, plough his fields, be used in harness, pack his merchandise to market, win races for him, and be trusted with his daughter.

The Cob was used for pack and riding in both world wars. It was crossed with the Thoroughbred to produce good hunters, played its part in the development of the Hackney and even of the Fell pony, and has had outstanding influence in the development of trotting horses all over the world.

PONY OF THE AMERICAS

Origin: United States.
Height: 11.2–13hh.
Color: Appaloosa (showing any of six color patterns).
Character: Willing, gentle, versatile; ideal for the young rider.
Physique: A miniature Appaloosa horse, displaying style, substance and symmetry. Arab-type head, concave face, large eyes, pointed ears. Good shoulder, deep chest, short, muscular back, rounded body, hindquarters lengthy and well muscled. Legs clean, and short in the cannon bone. Good feet. Neck slightly arched, head held proudly. Gay tail carriage. Action

Welsh Cob

Pony of the Americas

smooth in all its paces, the walk being straight with a long, easy stride, the trot balanced and free.

The Pony of the Americas is one of the very few breeds to be certain of its origin, no doubt because it is one of the newest. It began in 1956, when Mr Leslie L. Boomhower, a horse-breeder living in Mason City, Iowa, crossed a Shetland stallion on an Appaloosa mare and got a very attractive miniature Appaloosa colt, which he called Black Hand (pictured on page 67). Black Hand was so successful in the show ring, and so much generally admired by those who appreciated a good children's pony, that he became the foundation sire of a new breed.

The Pony of the Americas quickly became popular. It now has its own Stud Book, with P.O.A. Clubs in 24 States and in Canada, and by the end of 1971 12,598 ponies were registered. Foals are provisionally included in the register, but it is not until the ponies are 3 years old that they can offically qualify for the Stud Book. Qualification is on the basis of height, which must not be less than 11.2hh and must not exceed 13hh, on type, which is precisely laid down, and on coloring, which must conform to one of the recognized Appaloosa patterns. Examinations for registry are carried out by Club inspectors or by veterinary surgeons.

The Pony is intended as a versatile mount for a young rider up to 16 years of age. It has proved itself successful on trail rides, as a show jumper, and in children's races.

CHINCOTEAGUE AND ASSATEAGUE

Origin: United States – two islands off the Virginian and Maryland coasts.
Height: About 12hh.
Color: All colors; pinto is commonest.
Character: Stubborn and intractable, though with careful training they sometimes make good children's ponies.
Physique: In photographs that are not to scale they are easy to mistake for horses of a "common" lightweight type. The build is that of a small horse rather than a pony, and they do not have "pony" heads.

No one really knows where these ponies came from, or can account for their surprising presence on two American islands to which the horse is not indigenous. Legend claims that a boat carrying Moorish ponies from North Africa to Peru was shipwrecked off the coast of Virginia in early colonial times, and that some of these ponies swam to Assateague and Chincoteague, which are separated by only a narrow channel of sea. Here they survived unknown to man for a very long time (easy enough on Assateague, which is uninhabited).

Since their discovery by man they are said to have become better-looking: nothing to do with basking in their own reflected beauty, but more likely due to a rumored introduction of Welsh stallions to the wild herd, or perhaps to new blood of another kind.

Every year, on the last Thursday and Friday in July, Assateague ponies are rounded up and swum across the channel to Chincoteague, where ponies from both islands are sold by auction.

GALICENO

Origin: Mexico.
Height: 12–13.2hh.
Color: Bay, black, sorrel, dun, gray.
Character: Highly intelligent, versatile, brave and gentle.
Physique: Built like a small, compact, narrow horse. Intelligent head with a bold eye; narrow chest, and often upright shoulder; short, straight back; legs fine and hard and long in the gaskin; small, well-shaped feet. They have a natural running walk, a fast gait unusual in a pony.

Ancestors of this small horse are thought to have come from Galicia, in Spain, possibly among the 16 horses landed on the American mainland when Cortes invaded Mexico from Cuba, and probably of the Garrano or Minho breed. Refinement to its present type is thought to owe more to natural evolution than to selective breeding by man.

It is used for ranch work and for light transport, and its alert and kindly disposition has led it to excel in competitions. It is quick to learn, is hardy, and has stamina. It was first imported into the United States, where it is widely popular, as recently as 1959.

Galiceno

INDONESIAN PONIES

A variety of native pony breeds are to be found in the islands of Indonesia. All of them are small, and many are of primitive type, though there are a few who have been improved with Arab blood. They share the distinction of being able to work in the tropical heat. They are important to the economy of the country, and are widely used in agriculture as well as being one of the principal means of transport.

TIMOR: These, the smallest of the Indonesian ponies, come from the island of Timor, the most southerly of the Indonesian islands and the nearest to the Australian mainland. They have been exported to Australia and New Zealand, where they are much admired for their abundant common sense (several horse authorities have been impressed enough to call it wisdom), for their willingness and for their endurance.

They stand about 11hh, are usually dark in color (though one famous expert, R. S. Summerhays, refers to "chocolate body, cream spots and cream mane and tail suggesting the Appaloosa type"), are finely-built, and in good specimens display a decent depth of girth and a strong back and hindquarters. They are sure-footed and exceptionally agile, and despite their smallness are strong enough to work on cattle round-ups, carrying full-grown men. Apart from stock work, they are widely used in harness and are popular as children's riding ponies.

JAVA: A slightly-built little animal, ugly enough to make a horseman wince, it works all day in the tropic sun pulling *sados*, the two-wheeled traps commonly in use as a taxi service. Often it pulls a full load, always willingly, and it is remarkable for its strength and apparent tirelessness. It stands around 12.2hh, comes in most colors, and originates from Java.

BALI: A primitive breed, commonly showing the dun, dark points and dorsal stripe and occasionally the upright mane of the primeval pony. It stands 12–13.1hh, and is a strong, economical worker often used as a pack pony.

GAYOE: The Gayoe pony, from the north end of Sumatra, is heavier-built than the Batak and lacks its fire and speed.

BATAK (OR DELI): These Sumatran ponies have been bred selectively in proper studs, and as a result have a touch of elegance above the other island breeds. They are still common in type; but imported Arab stallions crossed with chosen local mares, some of them imported from other islands, have helped enormously to improve the Batak pony. It is now a relatively-handsome, spirited breed, sweet to handle and cheap to keep. There are no special colors for it — it seems to breed in most shades — and it stands 12–13hh.

Timor

Java

The Indonesian government, appreciating the importance of good ponies to the national economy, have encouraged selective breeding on Sumatra and are now exporting Bataks to other Indonesian islands to improve the native types.

SUMBA: A primitive breed from the island of Sumba, very closely related to the Sumbawa. It is usually dun, with the dark points and dorsal stripe common in ancient breeds. It stands about 12.2hh and is tough, willing and intelligent.

Sumba ponies are used in dancing competitions. Ridden bareback and reinless by young boys, controlled by the father's lunge rein on a halter, they dance to tom-tom rhythms. Bells are attached to their knees. In the intensity of the dance their eyes are said to get bigger and to glow. Dancing ponies are judged on elegance and lightness; barebacked ponies with heavy heads and stringy tails responding with laid-back ears to the sound of a drum. They are generally ridden in bitless bridles.

SUMBAWA: The agile pony of Sumbawa much resembles the Sumba.

SANDALWOOD: This pony, also from the islands of Sumba and Sumbawa, is of a finer type than most of the national breeds. It is named for Sumba's joint-biggest export (the other one is ponies), and is used in bareback racing. It is a fast, fine-coated pony which rarely sweats. It has a small, fine head, good eye, good, deep chest, hard legs, and is noted for its burnished coat. It stands 12.1–13.1hh, and its coloring is various.

MANIPUR

Origin: Assam – Manipur.
Height: 11–13hh.
Physique: Sturdy, sure-footed pony, thought from its appearance to have both Asiatic Wild Horse and Arab ancestors. Alert head, gaily carried; deep chest and well-sprung ribs; clean, hard legs; high-set tail.

Polo is a game which has been popular in Asia for almost 2,000 years, though with the decline of the Moghul empire it lost its vogue in India and would have died out had it not been for continued enthusiasm in the hill states of the Himalayas and Assam. The Western fondness for the game came about through its discovery by English planters who worked in Assam in the 1850s and who took to the local game with relish. The ponies they rode were Manipuris; and thus Manipur ponies, in Western eyes, are the original polo ponies. They are still used for the game in their home-land, though in Europe and America they have been succeeded by much bigger, faster animals.

Ponies have been bred in Manipur since time out of mind, though the breed must have undergone the gradual changes and refinements (or degeneracies) common to native breeds all over the world. There are

Batak (or Deli)

Sumba

records of polo having been locally introduced by the King of Manipur in the 7th century, when the game was played on ponies bred in his state.

Manipur ponies are claimed as the mounts of the all-conquering State cavalry which once terrorized northern Burma, though it is open to doubt whether these ponies actually were Manipuris or were simply ponies which came from Manipur. Writing in 1896 about the successes of the Manipuri cavalry, Major-General Sir James Johnstone says, "Manipur in olden days possessed a famous breed of ponies, larger and better bred than the so-called Burmese ponies that came from the Shan States. On these ponies were mounted the formidable cavalry that in the last century made Manipur feared throughout Upper Burma . . ." which places a big question mark above the historical identities of both these breeds, since today's Manipuri is smaller than the modern Burma pony.

BURMA (SHAN)

Origin: Burma.
Height: About 13hh.
Physique: Strong, active, unimpressive-looking pony similar to the smaller Manipuri.

The Burma pony, also known as the Shan, is bred mainly by the hill tribes in the Shan States of East Burma. Although neither fast nor quickly-responsive it was used by British officers stationed in Burma as a polo pony, surely a case of making desperate use of available material.

KATHIAWARI AND MARWARI

Origin: India.
Height: 14–15hh.
Color: Any – chestnut, bay, brown, gray, piebald, skewbald and cream are common.
Character: Uncertain temper. Amazing toughness and endurance.
Physique: Light-framed, narrow pony, hardy and able to live on next to nothing. The tips of the ears point inwards so sharply that when pricked they almost touch. Tendency to sickle hocks. A fairly widespread Arab influence, which breed figures prominently in its ancestry, is apparent.

Kathiawari ponies, from the Kathiawar peninsula on the north-west coast, and Marwaris, from Rajputana, are so much alike that there is nothing but repetition to be gained from treating them as separate breeds. They are descended from indigenous Indian ponies crossed with Arab blood, said to result from the shipwreck of a cargo of Arab horses on the west coast, the survivors running wild and breeding with the natives.

The less aristocratic of the two Marwari and Kathiawari ancestors, the common country-bred pony, is a wretched bag of bones, very narrow, standing roughly 13hh. It is found all over India, thriving with the toughness of a goat. (Illustrated on page 76.)

Manipur

Burma (Shan)

Kathiawari and Marwari

SPITI

Origin: India — Himalayan Mountains.
Height: 12hh.
Color: Usually gray.
Character: Intelligent, alert, tireless; not always of a good disposition.
Physique: A strong, thickset pony, sure-footed and up to weight. The head is intelligent and sharp-eared, set on a thick, short neck, the back short and strong. It has ample hindquarters and sturdy shoulders, legs short with plenty of bone, and hard, round feet.

The Spiti pony is bred in the high ranges of the Himalayas and does not do well in the heat of the plains. It is used as a pack pony on the unnerving mountain passes, and is prized by its principal breeders, the Kanyats, for whom it provides one of the main sources of income in trade with neighbouring states. Its kinship to the ponies of Tibet is obvious from its appearance.

BHUTIA

This pony, also from the Himalayas, is a larger but very similar version of the Spiti. It stands 13—13.2hh.

Spiti

Tibetan (Nanfan) (Text over page)

TIBETAN (NANFAN)

Origin: Tibet.
Height: Average 12.2hh.
Color: All colors.
Character: Intelligent, active, enduring and courageous.
Physique: Head intelligent and alert. Body strong, compact, with tail set on low on strong hindquarters. Short, strong legs with plenty of bone. Well-shaped feet. Thick mane and tail.

The Tibetan pony, also called Nanfan, is an all-purpose breed used for riding, agricultural and pack work. It is descended from Chinese and Mongolian ponies, and is closely related to the Spiti and Bhutia ponies of northern India, whom it resembles. (Illustrated on page 77.)

MONGOLIAN

Origin: Mongolia.
Height: 12.2–14hh.
Color: Usually black, brown, bay, dun.
Character: Enormously enduring.
Physique: Thick-set and compact. Heavy head with small eye and short, thick ears. Short, thick neck, deep chest, a short, strong back. Good quarters, and tail set fairly high and thick-haired at the roots. Strong legs with plenty of bone, and round, hard feet. Abundant mane and tail. Extremely hardy, they can – and generally do – survive on poor fare, and little of it.

The above description of the Mongolian pony should be taken only as a rough generalisation, since ponies approximating to this pattern are found all over Mongolia, Tibet and China and little effort is made by breeders to conform to type. Though stallions are usually selected, trouble is seldom taken to regulate the quality of the mares they breed to.

These are working ponies, bred in large numbers by nomadic tribes, surviving as best they can on whatever they can forage. They are used for a broad range of work – for herding, riding, carting, in agriculture, as pack ponies; and when not suitable for these tasks, and sometimes even when they are, they supply meat or milk for their masters. The mares are milked for three months after foaling, and the milk is made into cheese or fermented into *kumiss* on equine dairy farms. It is thought that yogurt was a Mongol invention made originally from mares' milk.

In a region as vast as the one covered by the Mongolian pony it is natural that many variations have developed, some because of differences in climate and fodder and some due to imported blood or selective breeding. Among them are:

Wuchumutsin, a more refined Mongolian type reared on rich grassland;
Heilung Kiang, having a large head with a slightly convex face;

Mongolian

Hailar, Sanho and *Sanpeitze,* which carry the blood of imported Russian stallions and stand 14–15hh;
Ili, a Russian-Mongolian cross standing 14.2–15hh, useful as a riding and pack animal.

The Mongolian is one of the most antique of all pony types. Its influence is apparent in breeds throughout Asia and its extent is due to the nomadic and warlike habits of the Mongols, who took vast herds of ponies on their travels as a *remuda.* Even today Outer Mongolia has more horses per head of human population than anywhere else in the world.

ASIATIC/MONGOLIAN WILD HORSE, *Equus Przewalskii Przewalskii Poliakov*

Origin: Mongolia.
Height: 12.1–14.1hh.
Color: Dun, usually with dark points and a mealy muzzle. Often lighter-colored round the belly, zebra stripes on forearms, hocks and gaskins. Dorsal stripe.
Character: Extremely brave. Great powers of endurance.
Physique: Primitive pony type. Large, broad head with long ears, often on a ewe neck. Short, upright mane, thin tail. Upright shoulder, strong back and loins, poor hindquarters. Strong legs with short pasterns, long feet. Immensely tough, survives rough climate and poor fare.

The wild horse of the Mongolian steppes was discovered by Colonel N. M. Przewalski in 1881. It lives in the Tachin Schara Nuru Mountains (the Mountains of the Yellow Horses) on the western fringe of the Gobi Desert. Very few remain today, as it has been hunted near to extinction. It is protected by the Mongolian, Russian and Chinese governments, and its biggest hope for survival lies not in its native habitat but in European and American zoos, where roughly 200 specimens (more than four times the number thought to exist in the wild) are being carefully bred.

The Asiatic Wild Horse is thought to be one of the basic breeds from which all horses have evolved. It has changed little since the Ice Age, which in the last few hundred years must have been due not so much to lack of opportunity for outcrossing with strangers but to its inhospitable habitat and its equally inhospitable views on intruders. In its feral state stallions and even two-year-old colts will attack and kill invading males long before they get near the mares, and runaway domestic mares are usually insufficiently hardy to withstand the extreme conditions in which it lives.

RUSSIAN PONIES

There are a number of closely-related breeds in the Baltic States, all of them extremely hardy, frugal, and strong and very enduring. Most are partly descended from the Klepper, a light draught type from Estonia; and it comes as a curious jolt to discover that "Klepper" is apparently not the name of a breed but is the local word for "nag". This is typical of the stumbling blocks encountered in trying to trace the history of all the purebred breeds and the confusion is increased by the intercultural smog that hangs over most Soviet breeds that are seldom seen in the West.

Information about the Baltic breeds often conflicts, but a picture emerges of a number of sturdy Northern forest types, very similar in appearance to the Polish Konik. Among them are the two following breeds.

VIATKA

Origin: USSR.
Height: 13–14hh.
Color: Dark colors. Dun, roan, gray are the most common. Many have a dorsal stripe, and slight zebra stripes on forelegs are not uncommon.
Physique: Longish head with wide, slightly concave, forehead. Muscular neck set into strong, deep chest with sloping shoulders. Broad, straight back with well-sprung ribs. Powerful hindquarters. Legs short with plenty of bone, the forelegs set wide apart and the hind often sickle-hocked. Thick mane and tail. Action short and active. Extremely frugal, and possessed of great stamina.

The Viatka is an attractive all-purpose pony, used mainly for light agricultural work and to pull *troikas* (sleighs drawn by three horses abreast). Originally from the Viatsky territory, it is now bred mainly in the Udmurt republic and the Kirov district, where State studs control the purity of the breed. Minor

Asiatic/Mongolian Wild Horse

Viatka

variations, named for the regions from which they originate, are the Obwinski and the Kasanski.

ZEMAITUKA

Origin: USSR.
Height: 13–14hh.
Color: Generally dun with dorsal stripes.
Character: Intelligent, willing, energetic, vast stamina.
Physique: Medium-sized head, straight face, wideset, intelligent eyes, rather small ears. Short, muscular neck, shoulder somewhat upright, powerful front. Straight back with well-sprung ribs, sloping quarters. Legs strong and clean, though light of bone. Hard, well-shaped feet.

The Zemaituka, descended centuries ago from the Asiatic Wild Horse crossed with the Arab, is one of the toughest ponies to be found anywhere. It can live on fodder that most ponies would not consider edible, survive the harshest climatic conditions, and still do 40 miles a day.

BASHKIRSKY

Origin: USSR.
Height: Average 13.2hh.
Color: Bay, chestnut, dun.
Character: Calm, good-natured. Very hardy, with great endurance.
Physique: Strong, sturdy body, strong neck and prominent withers. Long back, low-set tail. Abundant mane and tail. Legs short and strong, feet small and hard.

There are two types of Bashkirs, the Mountain and the Steppe, the Mountain type being very slightly smaller and more suitable for riding. The breed has been improved by crossing with riding horses (Budyonny and Don) in the south, and with harness horses (Trotters and Ardennes) in the west and north. Bashkirs go equally well under the saddle or harnessed to sleighs. Stallions and geldings are mainly used for these purposes, while mares are frequently milked for the production of *Kumiss*, a drink which is considered to have medicinal as well as alcoholic qualities. In Bashkiria they have been milked since the beginning of history, and a modern mare yields about 2,000 litres (440 gallons) of milk during a lactation period of 7–8 months.

Bashkirs are famous for their powers of endurance. A troika of Bashkirs is reputed to travel as much as 75 miles a day over snow (even if this is a wild exaggeration, it must rest on a most impressive fact).

KAZAKH

Origin: USSR – Kazakhstan.
Height: 12.2–13.3hh.
Color: Mainly bay, chestnut, gray or black. Sometimes odd-colored or dun.

Zemaituka

Bashkirsky

Character: Willing and enduring. Ideal long-distance pony.
Physique: Typical Central Asian pony, similar to the Mongolian, to which it is related. Short-backed, deep-chested, with very hard legs and feet.

Bred over a wide area, it varies in height and refinement of type according to the severity of the climate. The more elegant Kazakhs owe their improvement to the introduction of Don blood. Some Kazakhs amble rather than trot, and these are especially valued as riding ponies because the gait is smooth and comfortable. These steppe ponies are exceptionally hardy, able to endure extremes of heat and cold and to forage for themselves in knee-deep snow, or pick a living on the edge of the desert.

Kazakhs come from a region in which the horse has always been important. Seventh-century burial mounds, recently excavated, show that Kazakhstani nomads were buried with their ponies. These men depended on their horses for food and drink as well as for transport, and a study of the bones discovered shows that the ancient Kazakhstani ponies were much like their modern counterparts in size and build.

Nowadays, Kazakhs are still used to produce milk, and a mare will yield roughly 10 litres a day. This is usually made into the alcoholic beverage *Kumiss*. Young animals are fattened up for meat and are generally slaughtered when they reach a weight of about 1,000lb.

Kazakhs are used as cow ponies. They also make good cavalry animals when crossed with quality horses such as the Don, Budyonny or Akhal-Teke. Their endurance is such that they can travel 300 kilometres in 24 hours, and this accounts for their success in Russian equestrian sports such as the long-distance test which is called the *baiga*.

TARPAN *Equus Przewalskii Gmelini Ant*

Origin: Caucasian and eastern European, latterly Poland.
Height: About 13hh.
Color: Mouse dun to brown, with dark brown dorsal stripe. Wide, dark stripe down center of mane and tail with lighter hairs on each side, giving a variegated "streaked blonde" effect depending on which way the hair falls. Zebra stripes may appear on forelegs and inner thighs, and there are sometimes stripes on the body. Winter coat occasionally white, as in feral Arctic animals, when living in a very cold climate.
Character: Independent, brave (Tarpan stallions will attack domestic stallions which threaten their mares and fight to the death, often successfully), intractable, tenacious.
Physique: Long, broad head; slightly concave face, widening at nostrils. Longish ears on a short, thick neck stemming from good shoulders. Back long, quarters thin and sloping, legs fine and hard. Tarpan are extremely hardy and exceptionally fertile. Never known to abort, never seem to catch the common diseases, and when injured will heal without infection.

The Tarpan is a controversial breed, since some people feel that it became extinct at the end of the last century. It is reported that the last wild Tarpan was killed in 1879, near Askania Nova, Russia, and that the last Tarpan in captivity died in 1887. It is also reported that around 1887 the Polish government, dismayed at the passing of the Tarpan, collected a number of animals which appeared extremely Tarpan-like from peasant farms and turned these animals loose in the forest reserves of Bialowlieza and Popielno. Thus there is an argument about whether the breed has been "preserved" or "restored".

The appearance of the Tarpan suggests that the breed is probably pure, or so close to purity as makes no difference. It is an Ice Age horse. Eons ago it was widespread in Europe and western Asia, and it is therefore the base of many of the primitive breeds of horse and so is the ancestor of the more sophisticated breeds which were developed from primitive crosses. Thus, with Przewalski's Horse, it became the foundation of the modern warmbloods.

It seems that the Tarpan divided into two groups, one wandering in eastern Europe and the other grazing the steppes of the Ukraine. Thousands of years ago both groups were hunted for food; much as deer were hunted, but with a good deal more ruthlessness because the Tarpan stallion would attack his domestic rival ferociously. Tarpan meat was regarded as a great delicacy, so much in demand that by the end of the 18th century the breed had been hunted almost to extinction. Meanwhile, peasants who wanted cheap ponies had started to catch and train the Steppe Tarpan.

Tarpan

Today, Tarpan survive in a semi-wild state at Popielno, where a famous domesticated herd is kept, and are sometimes found in zoos or wildlife parks in various parts of the world.

There is a Mongolian legend of Tarpan dealing with Torguls, a human tribe descended from a Tarpan stallion. On the day of the birth of Torgut, son of lovely Irgit and magnificent Tarpan, stallions, mares and foals come from all points of the compass to witness the event. After a fierce fight with wolves, in which the stallions rout 20,000 of them, Tarpan, immortalized, trots proudly away with the young prince on his back.

HUÇUL

Origin: Poland — Carpathian Mountains.
Height: 12.1–13.1 hh.
Color: Usually dun, often with dark points, or bay.
Character: Sensible, docile, willing, hardy and enduring.
Physique: Strong, primitive pony with a Tarpan head and powerful body. General appearance pleasing and symmetrical, though the pony is sometimes cow-hocked.

This pony comes chiefly from the Huçulie district of the Carpathians. It is thought to stem mainly from Tarpan stock, and there are those who believe its ancestry to be so pure that they call it the Forest Tarpan. It is now selectively bred on several studs, and in the last century a great deal of Arab blood has been infused into it.

The Huçul is widely used as a work pony on farms throughout the higher land of southern Poland. It makes a splendid pack and draught animal, sure-footed enough for the most difficult country and of willing and untiring personality. Occasionally it is ridden, but this is not its main line of employment.

There are said to be three types of Huçul, though these have now interbred to a point of hazy distinction. They are, or were, the Przewalski Huçul, the Bystrzec Huçul and the Tarpan Huçul.

KONIK

Origin: Poland.
Height: About 13.1 hh.
Color: All shades of dun, usually with dorsal stripe. Some are said to grow white winter coats.
Character: Tough, independent pony, willing and good-natured.
Physique: A strong, well-proportioned pony very similar to the Huçul, to which it is closely related. It is extremely robust, and can thrive on poor fare. Exceptionally long lifespan and high fertility. Often cow-hocked.

This near relative of the Tarpan, one of the foundation breeds of eastern Europe, has influenced most of the Polish and Russian horses and ponies.

Huçul

Konik

It combines the toughness and frugality of the Tarpan with a kindly disposition and willingness to learn that makes it easy to train and a productive worker. It is as important to the economy of lowland farmers as the Huçul is to the hill farmers, and is so much in demand as a work pony both in Poland and in neighboring countries that it is widely bred by farmers and on State studs.

"Konik" means "small horse".

BOSNIAN

Origin: Yugoslavia — Bosnia-Herzegovina.
Color: Dun, brown, chestnut, gray, black.
Character: Tough, affectionate, very intelligent.
Physique: Compact mountain pony of the Tarpan type, not unlike the Huçul. Hardy, sturdy and enduring.

The Bosnian is the most widespread and important of the pony breeds in the Balkan states. Something like 400,000 of them are employed in Yugoslavia as farm and pack workers, and sometimes as riding ponies. In recognition of their quality, and with the intention of keeping up the great demand, they are carefully bred by the State; only chosen stallions are allowed to cover mares. To maintain the breed's excellence as pack ponies all stallions have to pass a test requiring them to carry a load of roughly 220lb for ten miles. This has been achieved in 71 minutes.

The Bosnian is yet another example of the basic Tarpan type which has been improved with Arab blood.

FJORD (WESTLANDS)

Origin: Norway.
Height: 13–14.2hh.
Color: All shades of dun, characteristically cream or yellow, with dorsal stripe and often stripes on forelegs and thighs. Mane and tail are black and silver, the central ridge of the mane being dark and the outside hairs light-colored.
Character: Hardworking, tireless, gentle, sociable and self-willed.
Physique: Smallish, well-shaped head with broad forehead, wideset eyes and small ears. Upright mane, characteristically cut on a crescent about 4in high at the center, on a short, thick neck that merges into the shoulder without much definition at the point of join and into the back with almost no visible withers. Body immensely powerful and muscular with a long back and rounded hindquarters. Short, sturdy legs with feather on the heels, sloping pasterns, and hard, long feet. Sure-footed and extremely hardy.

The Fjord pony is one of the few breeds to have kept its identity recognizably throughout the centuries. It has changed little from the horse the Vikings bred and used for horse-fights (see Iceland pony, page 57), and is still bred

Bosnian

Fjord (Westlands)

all over its ancestral Norwegian homeland. It flourishes throughout the other Scandinavian countries, and is especially popular in Denmark, to which it has been exported in quantity during the last century.

It is a stoutly-built, primitive sort of pony, fond of company, and with a great deal of charm in its appearance and personality. It is indispensable in high mountain areas that are too steep or too cold for the tractor or the lorry, and because of this it seems likely to endure as a working pony. It will pull a plough or a cart, will pack a load on rugged mountain paths, or serve as a pleasant, weight-carrying riding pony; and additionally it is frugal and cheaply fed, indifferent to cold, and endlessly hardworking.

HAFLINGER

Origin: Austria and Bavaria — Tirol.
Height: About 14hh.
Color: Chestnut with flaxen mane and tail. Other colors rare.
Character: Docile, adaptable, frugal, hardworking and long-lived.
Physique: Medium-sized head with pointed muzzle, kind, alert eye, open nostrils, small ears. Well-muscled body, wide-chested and deep-girthed, long, broad back, strong loins and quarters. Short legs with plenty of bone. Round, hard feet. Action free and elastic with a long, smooth stride.

These ponies are reared on mountain pastures and are left to mature until they are four years old before they are broken in, which may have something to do with their reputed ability sometimes to work until they are 40. Certainly they have extremely long lives and are exceedingly strong in the limbs, heart and lungs. They are marvelous mountain ponies, splendid for riding as well as for harness and pack work, being sure-footed and tireless.

Haflingers possess Arab blood.

The brand of the Haflinger is an edelweiss (the Austrian national flower), with an "H" in the center.

AVELIGNESE

Origin: Italy.
Height: 13.3–14.3hh.
Color: Chestnut with blond mane and tail.
Character: Gentle and easy to train, tough and long-lived.
Physique: Strong, muscular working pony with a comparatively delicate, pointed head with wideset eyes. Strong shoulders with wide chest, a long back with powerful loins and hindquarters. Legs short with plenty of bone. Sloping pasterns with feather, large, hard hooves.

The Avelignese is a cousin of the Haflinger (both breeds are descended from the now-extinct Avellinum-Haflinger) and is quite like it to look at, though a little larger and heavier. It is a kindly, sure-footed animal, seldom subject to illness, and is popular as a pack horse in the Alps and the Apennines. It is

Haflinger

Avelignese

also valued for light agricultural work. It is said to contain a considerable quantity of Oriental blood, though its appearance does not lend much substance to this claim.

CAMARGUAIS

Origin: France – Camargue.
Height: Roughly 14hh.
Color: Gray.
Physique: Fine, Oriental-type head, broad between the eyes and rather long in the face. Some tendency to upright shoulder, but chest good and body short and strong in the loins. Hindquarters slight, with a penchant for goose rumps. Legs fine, with good bone, and feet broad and large. Thick mane and tail.

This breed is thought to be very old and to possess Oriental blood, the former unproven but probable and the latter likely from the general look of it. The ponies mostly live wild in the Rhône delta, but can work well as cow ponies or trekking ponies.

MERENS

Origin: France – Ariège river hill region.
Height: About 13.3hh.
Color: Black.
Physique: A compact, sturdy breed with a heavy head. Abundant bone. Full mane and tail.

The Mérens is a strong working type, running half-wild in the high foothills of the Ariège. It is probably an ancient breed, and probably has Oriental roots.

FELL

Origin: England – Westmorland and Cumberland.
Height: 13–14hh.
Color: Usually black; occasionally bay, brown or gray. White markings rare, especially on legs, where they are considered undesirable.
Character: Lively, alert pony; an excellent ride and also, because strong and untiring, a good work pony.
Physique: Alert head, carried high, with short, pricked ears. Good, sloping shoulder. Muscular body with well-sprung ribs and strong loins. Strong, sloping hindquarters. Thick mane and tail, gay tail carriage. Hard, strong legs with some feather. Feet hard and round. It has a smooth, fast trot which it can keep up for many miles. Very hardy.

This all-purpose pony, nowadays almost exclusively used for riding, was

Camarguais

Fell

93

formerly a harness pony and farm worker in the uplands districts and a lead-mines pack pony. In the 17th and 18th centuries pack ponies were used to take lead from the mines to the coast — there were no roads suitable for heavy carts — and the Fell regularly carried 220lb for 30 miles and more day by day. It was also famous as a trotter during the 19th century. It could trot at up to 20 miles an hour for many miles without fatigue. It has great substance.

The Fell appears to stem from the Friesian horses introduced to Britain by the Romans (see Friesian, page 170), and from the now-extinct Galloway breed of the west Scottish lowlands, of which the 17th century writer Gervase Markham, in his book *The Horseman's Honour or the Beautie Of Horsemanship*, reports: "In Scotland there are a race of small nagges which they call Galloways or galloway nagges which for fine shape, easie pace, pure metall and infinit toughness are not short of the best nagges that are bred in any country whatsoever."

DALES

Origin: England — north country dales.
Height: 14–14.2hh.
Color: Jet black, bay, dark brown (locally known as heckberry). White markings other than a small star on the face or a white heel or coronet are unacceptable, since a white face, fetlock or hoof indicates a touch of Clydesdale ancestry.
Character: Sensible, quiet to handle. These qualities, combined with its great physical strength and sureness of foot, make it ideal for pony trekking, though its strength makes it a more suitable ride for adults than for children. Thrives on work.
Physique: Powerful body with muscular back and quarters. Head should be pony-like. Abundant mane and tail, feather on feet. Exceptionally strong, capable of carrying a 16-stone (224lb) rider or pulling a load weighing a ton.

A native of the eastern side of the Pennines, the Dales pony is very similar in appearance to its slightly smaller close relation, the Fell pony. Both are of Celtic descent, and have been used for hundreds of years by fell and dales farmers for carting and riding and all kinds of farm work. In the 17th and 18th centuries they worked as pack ponies, carrying lead from the mines to the coast.

Some outcrossing was done to improve the Dales pony for farm work and for transport. In the 19th century a famous Welsh Cob stallion, Comet, was brought to the dales to compete in trotting matches, which were a local sport. Comet, who could trot 10 miles in 33 minutes carrying 12 stone (168lb) on his back, was bred to the Dales mares with such unanimous approval that today every Dales pony traces back to this great Welsh Cob.

With the invention of heavy machinery and automobiles the Dales pony became redundant. Hundreds were slaughtered for meat, and by the early 1950s the breed was nearly extinct. It was saved by the advent of pony

Dales

trekking, and is now much used to carry tourists across country where, for centuries before, its ancestors carried the local doctor or the farmer on his way to market.

HIGHLAND

Origin: Scotland.
Height: Garron: About 14.2hh. Western Isles: 12.2–14.2hh.
Color: Usually varying shades of dun with dorsal stripe, often with black points or silver hairs in tail and mane. Also gray, chestnut (sometimes with blond mane and tail), bay, black.
Character: Intelligent, responsive, and very docile. It is a sensitive pony, giving its trust generously to a good owner but tending to be wary of strangers and easily soured by bad treatment.
Physique: There are two types of Highland pony, the Western Isles and the Garron, or Mainland, variety. The Garron, bigger and stronger than the Islands type, is a powerful, well-made animal with a short, deep head with open nostrils, bright, intelligent eyes and short ears. Head well-carried on strong, cresty neck of medium length; shoulders powerful, chest and girth deep and roomy. Back short, with well-sprung ribs and strong loins, hindquarters full and powerful. Legs short, hard and strong, with plenty of bone, and thick feather at the fetlock joint. Hard, broad hooves. Long, thick tail, well set on, and plentiful mane. Action is straight and free and well-balanced, though it has a tendency to be "on the forehand". It is a sturdy, hardy pony, and very sure-footed.

The Western Isles type, grouped into two divisions according to height (those 12.2–13.2hh and 13.2–14.2hh), is a smaller and finer-limbed version of the Garron.

The Highland pony is traditionally associated with deer stalking. It is sure-footed enough to carry a deer's carcase on the steep and slippery slopes of the Scottish glens, and so docile and trusting that a hunter can fire a gun from its back.

Of the two types of Highlander the Garron is the type with which the name Highland Pony is most generally associated. It is simply a scaled-up version of the Western Isles type, developed during the last century in response to the need for a strong working pony which had the weight to pull or carry a big load. The Garron is the biggest and strongest of all the British pony breeds, and has been known to carry at a canter (in a circus act) seven adult riders at a combined estimated weight of 60 stone (840lb) without any apparent difficulty.

Highland ponies contain Arab blood; also some French blood and a bit of Clydesdale is thought to have contributed to the Garron. The smaller Western Isles type is an excellent children's riding pony, while the bigger Garron – in the past the crofter's pony of all work as well as the stalker's friend – today makes a first-class trekking pony.

CONNEMARA

Origin: Ireland – Connaught Province.
Height: 13–14hh.
Color: Originally dun with dorsal stripe and black points. Now more commonly gray; also black, brown, bay.
Character: Intelligent, tractable and exceptionally kind. Excellent children's riding pony.
Physique: Alert head, well-carried; good, medium-length neck on strong, sloping shoulders. Deep girth, long, compact body with strong, often sloping, hindquarters. Legs are short and hard, with good bone. Hard feet. Action free and comfortable. Sure-footed and hardy, the Connemara is also an excellent jumper.

The Connemara is an ancient breed, probably of the same basic family as the Western Isles type of Highland pony. It has run wild in the mountains of the Irish west coast from beyond the memory of man, and was interbred quite considerably with Spanish jennets imported as a result of the wreck of the Spanish Armada in 1588. More recently Arab blood has been introduced, and latterly Arabs and small Thoroughbreds have been bred to Connemara mares and the offspring registered as Connemara; so that the breed has changed quite considerably and it is questionable how many "Connemara" ponies of today really deserve the name. Certainly dun, once the typical color of the Connemara, is becoming very scarce.

Until recent times the Connemara has been a multi-purpose pony, used

Highland

Connemara

to carry peat and turf, in harness, and for riding. Outcrosses of it have regularly produced good stock – it has almost certainly contributed to the famous Irish hunter, and crosses with Thoroughbred stallions have produced showjumpers of great ability, notably the international showjumper Dundrum (by the Thoroughbred stallion Little Heaven out of a Connemara mare) who, although only 14.3hh, could clear seven feet.

Like all native ponies the Connemara retains its type best when fed on poor keep, which makes it difficult for breeders with lush pasture to maintain the original pony character and restrict their ponies' height to the maximum of 14.2hh permitted by the English Connemara Pony Society. It seems generally agreed that Connemaras of the best hard, wiry type stand not much more than 13.2hh.

NEW FOREST

Origin: England – New Forest area of Hampshire.
Height: 12–14.2hh.
Color: Any color except piebald or skewbald.
Character: Intelligent, brave, willing, docile, very friendly, and quick to learn. Because the New Forest area – less a forest than an open expanse of common cross-hatched with roads and picnic places – is within handy reach of London and the densely-populated south east, the free-range pony is exposed to visitors from birth and grows up less shy of people and of man-created terrors such as traffic than any of the other British mountain and moorland breeds. For this reason it is the safest possible ride for children.
Physique: Because the New Forest pony is a mixture of many breeds which have been turned loose on the common over the centuries with no serious attempt to control the type until 1938, it comes in a wide range of sizes and shapes. However, under the watchful eye of the New Forest Pony Breeding and Cattle Society, a definite type is becoming recognized:

Rather large head with intelligent eye, well set on a shortish neck. Good shoulder, short back with deep girth and strong loins and hindquarters. Good, hard legs with short cannon bones and excellent feet. It is a hardy, thrifty pony with plenty of endurance.

The ponies are categorized into two types. Type A, lighter in bone than the bigger Type B, stands up to 13.2hh and is an excellent child's hunter and riding pony. Type B stands 13.2–14.2hh and is a suitable ride for a small adult.

More than a thousand years ago the area covered by the New Forest extended through southern England nearly as far west as Dartmoor and Exmoor, and so it is probable that the original New Forest pony was closely akin to those of the Devon and Somerset moors. The breed has been mixed with abundant new blood since those days, among it that of the Thoroughbred stallion Marske, sire of the unbeaten racehorse Eclipse. In 1765 Marske, who had amounted to little on the racetrack, was sold cheap to a Dorset farmer who used him to cover New Forest mares. Marske's obscurity as a farm stallion lasted for only 4 years. In 1769 Eclipse (foaled 1764) saw a racecourse for the first time and ran with such brilliant supremacy that his sire was quickly sought out and was sold away up to Yorkshire for £20. In the years 1852 to about 1890 Queen Victoria lent three Arab stallions to run wild in the Forest, and these must have had some effect upon improving the native ponies — though the degree of their effect would depend upon their personalities, since it is not the most beautiful stallion who covers the mares in the wild but the most determined and aggressive. In the last part of the 19th century Lord Arthur Cecil introduced to the Forest other native mountain and moorland breeds such as the Galloway and Welsh. Attempts to "improve" the New Forest pony with richer blood were not universally successful since the progeny was not necessarily able to cope with the sparse winter feed provided by the Forest. It seems logical that today's pony which continues to survive running wild all year round must owe the larger part of its ancestry to the other hardy British mountain and moorland breeds.

The New Forest is the most tractable of all the British riding ponies. It makes a splendid hunter, and seems impervious to any sort of traffic. Unfortunately, this last quality permits it to wander without fear on the unfenced roads of the Forest and causes a high annual death and injury toll.

New Forest

HACKNEY PONY

Origin: England.
Height: 12.2–14.2hh.
Color: Usually bay, brown, chestnut, black.
Character: Active, honest, courageous, and possessed of great endurance.
Physique: True pony type. Pony head with prick ears, long neck, compact body with good shoulders and quarters, iron-hard legs and good feet. Action highly dramatic, the knees raised as high as they can go and the feet flung forward with an extravagant, rounded motion. Hocks brought up high under the body, with movement on all four feet straight and true. The effect of a hackney at the trot is one of flamboyance and brilliance.

The word *hackney* comes from the Norman French *haquenai*, which was applied in the Middle Ages to riding animals of the humblest caste ("He wened have repreved be Of theft or mordre if that he Had in his stable any Hakenay" – Chaucer, being rude about them). Quite why this derogatory word, which worked its way into *hack* = hireling in the sense of a wretch loaned out for a small sum, came to be applied to the highly-prized breed developed during the 19th century from the famous old Norfolk Roadster trotting horse by way of the Arab and Thoroughbred with help from Fell and Welsh ponies is not clear; but by the mid-19th century the Hackney was held in great esteem not only in the British Isles but also on the Continent, to which many of the best Hackneys were exported.

Hackney Pony

It is exclusively a harness pony, trotting with a wonderful, airy grace which makes it seem to fly over the ground. In the days before motorization it was very popular as a carriage pony, and because of its high price and smart appearance was valued as a prestige delivery pony by tradesmen who wanted to show their customers that they were successful. Fears that the car and truck would render it extinct have proved baseless. Although its numbers are much reduced, and only the best show types now have much value, the modern Hackney has become one of the most consistent crowd-drawers in the show ring.

Hackneys are also popular throughout North America, where they appear in the show ring with tails nicked to give an artificially high carriage. Though the American Hackney Horse Society Stud Book does not distinguish between horse and pony, the smaller American Hackneys of pony type, sometimes called "Bantam" Hackneys (some are bred as small as 11hh), must have definite pony character. Aside from harness work they are also used for riding and for showjumping, at which sport they were once much in demand in Great Britain because of the powerful muscular development of the hindquarters and legs.

(See also Hackney Horse, page 124.)

SABLE ISLAND

Origin: Canada — Sable Island.
Height: About 14hh.
Color: Usually chestnut (often dark), bay, brown, black, gray.
Physique: Strong, wiry animals, usually scrub type but occasionally handsome. Extremely hardy.

Sable Island, an Atlantic sandbank off the coast of Nova Scotia, grows no trees and no rich pastures. The two or three hundred ponies, descended from 18th-century New England stock, which live wild on the island survive without shelter or windbreak throughout winters which are often severe.

They are used in harness and as riding ponies.

BASUTO

Origin: South Africa — Basutoland.
Height: About 14.2hh.
Color: Chestnut, bay, brown, gray.
Character: Fearless and exceptionally self-reliant and enduring.
Physique: Sometimes a quality head, intelligent eye; lean, longish neck, often "ewe", on strong shoulder tending to the upright. Back on long side. Legs short and hard. Feet exceptionally hard. Amazingly sure-footed.

This pony, not native to Basutoland, derives from Arabs and Barbs imported by the Dutch East India Company in 1653 and from Arabs, Barbs,

Basuto

Persians and Thoroughbreds imported until early in the 19th century. This early cross-breeding of quality horses happened not in Basutoland but in Cape Province. It resulted in the Cape Horse, which crossed into Basutoland round about the 1830s by way of border raids and gradually deteriorated, through lack of interest and the demands of the hard, arid climate, into the Basuto pony.

An almost complete absence of cosseting in an inhospitable region has made the Basuto one of the toughest and bravest ponies in the world. It served extensively in the Boer War, has been used for racing and for polo, and can carry a full-grown man for 60 to 80 miles a day.

BALEARIC

Origin: Balearic Islands – Majorca.
Height: About 14hh.
Color: Bay, brown.
Physique: Fine head, often Roman-nosed, on short, arched neck. Upright mane. Body lean, and legs hard though light of bone. Hard feet. Action free and graceful.

This ancient Mediterranean breed, resembling the horses found on Greek coins, works with great docility on the small farms of Majorca and in harness for the Palma tradesmen. It is a gently patient sort which will stand without restraint under the almond trees between the shafts of the typical wide-spanned, green-netted carts into which the almond crop is dropped. Often it wears a sun hat, its ears poking out on either side of the crown as it stands, half-dozing, waiting for the signal to move to another tree.

NATIVE TURKISH

Origin: Turkey – Sivas.
Height: 14–14.2hh.
Color: Bay, brown, gray.
Character: Willing, and extremely enduring and hardy.
Physique: Plain head with long ears on short, thick neck, body short and strong. Legs strong with good bone, of medium length, and hard feet.

Native ponies are widely used in Turkey for all kinds of farm work, as pack ponies, in harness, and for riding. They are tough, enduring animals of no special distinction except for their readiness to do any job that is asked of them.

AUSTRALIAN

Origin: Australia.
Height: 12–14hh.
Character: Intelligent, game and enduring.
Physique: Arab head with intelligent eye and small, pricked ears, carried proudly on longish neck. Good, sloping shoulder, short back with deep girth and well-sprung ribs. Rounded hindquarters with tail well set on and gaily carried. Short, clean legs and hard feet. Action free, straight and smooth.

The Australian pony, almost unknown outside its own continent, is an elegant little animal stemming mainly from imported Welsh Mountain and Arab stock with infusions of Timor, Shetland, Exmoor and Thoroughbred blood.

HORSES: WARM BLOODED

WALER

Origin: Australia.
Height: Varies. About 16hh is preferred.
Color: All colors.
Character: Brave, sensible and enduring.
Physique: Varies considerably. The best have an alert head with straight face, wide nostrils, longish ears; neck well set on strong shoulders; good depth of girth, strong back and hindquarters; clean legs with plenty of bone and strong hocks.

Horses are not indigenous to Australia. The earliest forerunners of the Waler — one stallion, three mares, a colt and two fillies of predominantly Spanish blood — were brought from the Cape of Good Hope with the First Fleet of settlers in 1798. During the next few years other, better quality imports were brought from England into the early settled territories then collectively known as New South Wales, from which the name "Waler" derives.

The extensive rich pastureland and warm, dry climate of Australia was and is favorable to horse breeding, and the small numbers of early stock were easy to multiply. In 1810 Australia had 1,134 horses; in 1821 there were 4,564. Massive improvement with top quality Arab and Thoroughbred imports produced a horse which, during the first half of the 19th century, came close to being an Anglo-Arab in all but name. It was highly regarded as a saddle horse and was much in demand as a cavalry remount by the British Army in India.

The gold rush of the 1850s and 1860s was responsible for a rapid deterioration of the Waler. Farming was neglected and horses were allowed to roam fairly freely and often to breed as they chose, and in addition a demand for small draught horses to pack the gold encouraged many breeders to disregard the true saddle horse type. Not until the 1880s, when accumulated gold began to burn the pockets of the newly rich, did interest turn to luxury hobbies such as racing and the breeding of quality horses, and then it was that the Waler was regenerated.

As quality saddle stock, the Waler had its heyday early in the 20th century. Subsequent mechanization has led to a decline both in numbers and in consistency of quality, so that the Waler of today is more of a type than a breed. It had its finest hour during World War I, when more than 120,000 were exported for the Allied armies in India, Africa, Palestine and Europe. When the war was finished Australian quarantine laws made the repatriation of these horses impossible, and many were destroyed in the desert by an Australian government order. A bronze memorial in Sydney stands in memory of them today, erected

. . . by members of the Desert Mounted Corps and friends, to the gallant horses who carried them over the Sinai desert into Palestine, 1915–19. They suffered wounds, thirst, hunger, and weariness almost beyond endurance, but never failed. They did not come home.

BRUMBY

Origin: Australia.
Character: Genuine wild horse of considerable intelligence. Almost impossible to catch, and, once caught, almost impossible to train.
Height, color, physique: Varies widely. Usually a degenerated scrub horse.

"Brumby" is the Australian name for "wild horse". The origin of the name is not known, but it is thought to have come from one of three sources: from a pioneer horsebreeder called James Brumby, from "baroomby," the Queensland aboriginal word for wild, or from Baramba, the name of a station and creek in Queensland.

During the great gold rush of the mid-19th century many domestic horses were turned loose on the ranges, breeding freely and in many cases becoming inbred and deteriorating in quality. As is usual when domestic horses run wild only the most adaptable and the brainiest survived; but the Australian climate suits horses well, and Brumbies soon became so numerous that they became a threat to agriculture. Mechanization following World War I added to the problem when further quantities of unwanted domestic horses were loosed, and soon Brumbies were regarded as pests through the damage caused to pasture, fences, water holes and their perpetual invitation to station horses. Culling became necessary by gun, by "running" into traps, and by trapping through building concealed corrals along their favorite routes, and in the early 1960s Brumbies were hunted with jeeps,

Waler

with motor cycles and with light aircraft. Comparatively few remain; and these, when caught, are hard to train and scarcely worth the effort.

CRIOLLO

Origin: South America.
Height: 13.3–15hh.
Color: Preferred color dun with dark points, a dorsal stripe, a dark snippet on withers and slight zebra stripes on legs. Usually there are white markings on legs and face. Other common colors include red and blue roan, liver chestnut, palomino, mixed colors such as blue and white. Chestnut, gray, black and bay are also seen.
Character: Immensely tough, willing, and possessing outstanding endurance.
Physique: Compact, sturdy, handsome animal. Head short and broad, tapering to a fine, pointed muzzle, straight face with wide-set, expressive eyes, short pricked ears. Muscular neck set on a deep, strong shoulder with broad chest. Back short with well-sprung ribs and powerful loins. Rounded, muscular hindquarters. Legs short with excellent bone, short pasterns, small, hard feet.

South America produces one of the hardiest breeds of horse in the world – the little Criollo, mount of the gauchos of the great stock ranges of the central part of the continent. It appears, with slight variations in height and refinement of type, as the Criollo of Argentina and Uruguay, the Crioulo of Brazil, the Costeño and Morochuco types of Peru, the Caballo Chileno of Chile and the Llanero of Venezuela. Though some of the forenamed types are by now pretty well distinct from the basic Criollo type shown in the illustration, all are descended from the same Spanish stock imported by the Conquistadors in the 16th century. Refinements in the breed are due to variations in temperature and quality of pastureland, to being reared on the hills or in the plains, and to selective breeding for particular qualities according to the local requirements.

The basic blood is Andalusian, Barb and Arab; the smallness and toughness is due to some 300 years of rigorous natural selection during which herds of Criollos ran wild or semi-wild on the plains; and the curious range of sandy and dun colorings, unique in the Criollo, is held by many to have evolved as protective coloring in the wild.

In Argentina especially people take great pride in the Criollo's endurance, and stamina tests are held to select the best for breeding. An annual ride is conducted by breeders in which the horses must cover 470 miles in 15 days carrying 17 stone (242lb), with nothing to eat or drink along the way except such food as they can find for themselves during their periods of rest.

MANGALARGA

Origin: Brazil.
Height: Roughly 14.3hh.
Color: Bay, chestnut, gray, roan.
Physique: Rather long, alert head with intelligent eye. Strong, sloping shoulder, prominent withers, short back with strong loins, powerful, rounded hindquarters with tail low set on. Legs long, with good bone. A lighter-framed horse than the Criollo, being less stocky in the body and longer in the cannon bones and pasterns.

The breed is about 100 years old, and is the product of Andalusian and Portuguese Altér stallions used on Crioulo mares. The result is a riding horse of some elegance. In some instances it has an unusual gait called the Marcha, which is a comfortable rocking movement between a trot and a canter.

A similar but somewhat heavier breed called the Campolino exists in Brazil, useful under the saddle and also for light draught work. It has more depth of girth and chest than the Mangalarga, and is shorter in the pasterns and cannon bones. It was founded a century ago by Sr Cassiano Campolino.

PERUVIAN STEPPING HORSE

Origin: Peru.
Height: 14–15.2hh.
Color: Preponderantly bay and chestnut, but can be any color.
Character: Typical Criollo personality – enormous endurance, and thrives under stress.

Criollo

Mangalarga

Physique: Broad, deep chest, providing exceptional room for heart and lungs. Strong loins and quarters. Unusually long hind legs with great flexibility of the joints. Good bone, long pasterns, hard feet.

The Peruvian Stepping Horse, also called the Peruvian Paso, has a unique gait specially developed to carry a rider long distances with a minimum of fatigue. In the *paso* the forelegs move in an extravagant paddle while the hindlegs move in a long-striding straight line with the hindquarters held low and the hocks well under the horse. The action seems to be similar to the medieval gait called the amble which is now — and almost certainly to our disadvantage — unknown in Europe. Similarities to the paso exist in some of the gaits of North American horses such as the rack and the singlefoot, but it has no exact parallel. It is a gait that can be kept up untiringly by the horse, even on difficult country, and it is very easy on the rider. It has an average speed of about 11mph.

The Peruvian Stepper has been bred for 300 years, which explains its odd physical development. It is thought to have stemmed from three-quarters Barb and one-quarter Andalusian ancestry, but under the same pressures of climate, terrain and pasture which created the Criollo it has evolved into a distinctive South American Criollo type.

NATIVE MEXICAN

Origin: Mexico.
Height: Roughly 15hh.
Color: Any.
Physique: Small saddle horse of varying type, but basically a lean-framed animal with good shoulder, short back, strong loins and hindquarters, hard legs with plenty of bone, and hard feet.

The Mexican horse is thought to be a mixture of the breeds running wild in North and South America, possessing Andalusian, Arab, Criollo and Mustang blood and of course originally tracing to the horses of the Conquistadors. It is a tough, handy little animal, adapted by natural selection to a harsh climate, quick and flexible enough to be used for ranch work and brave enough to face a bull in the ring.

PASO FINO

Origin: Caribbean — Puerto Rico and equatorial South America.
Height: About 14.3hh.
Color: All colors.
Character: Gay, tractable, willing.
Physique: Strong small horse with Arab-type head, gaily carried. Short pricked ears, expressive eye and open nostrils. Good shoulder, short back with strong loins and quarters. Hard legs, light of bone, with short cannon bones and hard feet.

The Paso Fino exhibits three natural lateral four-beat gaits, a comfortable inherited characteristic which does not have to be taught but which appears in the foal at birth. The slowest and most collected gait is called the paso fino; then comes the paso corto, which covers long distances at a steady pace, and lastly there is the faster paso largo. It is believed that the gaits trace directly to early imported Spanish horses of the 16th century, and that apart from modifications and refinements to suit its new and varying climate, the Paso Fino remains similar to the mounts of the Spanish explorers. Strains developed separately in Puerto Rico, Peru and Colombia are now being merged in the United States into the American Paso Fino.

MUSTANG

Origin: United States.
Height: 14–15hh.
Color: All colors.
Character: Brave, independent and intractable.
Physique: Lightweight saddle horse of scrub type and usually plain appearance. Good bone, very hard legs and feet. Extremely hardy and thrifty.

The feral horse of North America, which used to roam the plains in large herds during the pioneering days of the country, is descended from Spanish horses brought by the Conquistadors which got loose or were captured by Indian tribes. Over a period of some 300 years of freedom they adapted themselves, by natural selection and by survival of the fittest, from quality Spanish stock to very tough, inelegant utility animals. They came in all colors, shapes and sizes. They were the ponies used by the Indians, and were also the original cow ponies.

Today the Mustang is on the decline, though its continued existence is likely because of government laws ensuring its protection and allotting to it specific areas of free range. It has been largely replaced on the ranches by range horses of better quality, and even the Bronco – the name given to the most intractable fighters among the wild Mustangs – is now being home bred for rodeo bucking competitions.

APPALOOSA

Origin: United States (probably).
Height: 14.2–15.2hh. Not less than 14hh.
Color: There are 6 basic patterns: frost, leopard, snowflake, marble, spotted blanket and white blanket, though many variations exist. The most common ground color is roan, though Appaloosas may be of any color provided that their spots conform to an accepted pattern. Other colors are, however, very unusual, with the exception of the horse having colored spots on a white ground. Skin round the nostrils, lips, and genitalia is mottled. White sclera round eye. Hooves sometimes vertically striped.

Character: Tractable disposition combined with speed, stamina, hardiness and great endurance. Handy and quick on its feet.

Physique: Compact, large-boned, with short, straight back. Wispy mane and tail (called "rat-tailed" or "finger-tailed"). Hooves hard (striped hooves claimed by some Appaloosa-fanciers to be more resilient than ordinary hooves).

The development of the Appaloosa is attributed to the Nez Percé Indians, who lived in the fertile north-western area of America now covered by the states of Washington, Oregon, and Idaho watered by the Palouse river. The name Appaloosa is a corruption of "Palouse horse" or "Palousy". In 1877 the Nez Percé were nearly wiped out in a 6-day battle with the US Army, and 61 years later the horses they had bred were recognized as an official breed. Though still chiefly to be found in western areas of the United States, the Appaloosa has grown so much in national popularity that it ranks as one of the half-dozen biggest breeds in America. It is internationally admired for its striking appearance, and is much in demand overseas as a circus horse.

The precise origins of the Appaloosa are obscure, since horses with similar markings appear in ancient Chinese and Persian art and in much earlier cave art at Pêche Merle. The claim that Appaloosas came to Nez Percé from Mexico through the agency of Cortés' importations from Spain in the 16th century is probably not far out, since all foundation American horses originate

Appaloosa: Spotted Blanket

Appaloosa: Leopard

Appaloosa: Blanket, Dark Mane

Appaloosa: Snowflake

Appaloosa: Raindrop

Appaloosa: Dark Foreparts

from Spanish stock. It is possible that the forerunners of the medieval Spanish Appaloosa were bred in Central Asia (hence the paintings), but here it begins to be necessary to distinguish between Appaloosa as a breed and Appaloosa as a color: throughout the world there are ponies with Appaloosa coloring who bear no physical resemblance to the quality cow-pony type of the recognized American breed. Whether the coloring of these widely-varied types indicates a common heredity or simply a spontaneous quirk of evolution remains a mystery.

PALOMINO

Origin: The United States is mainly responsible for the widespread interest in horses of the coat color known as Palomino, though horses of this coloring must have existed long before the United States began.

Height: As Palomino is not a breed but a color, the height varies. It can occur over the whole range of sizes, from small ponies to heavy draught horses. The Association of Palomino Horse Breeders of America, which is patiently trying to establish a breed, recognizes horses in the 14.2–15.3hh range provided that they conform to a good saddle type.

Color: Coat should be gold rather than chestnut or yellow, with no markings other than white on face or legs. Mane and tail white with not more than 15% dark or chestnut hair. Dark eyes.

Physique: Varies. The type preferred in America is that of a quality riding horse of an accepted American sort, such as the Quarter Horse or Morgan. In Britain, Palomino is more sought after in children's ponies of spirited appearance, such as Arab-Welsh Mountain crossbreds.

Although Palominos have been carefully bred in the United States for more than 40 years it is still not possible to breed true to color with any guarantee, and for this reason Palomino cannot yet be described as a breed. Persistent selective breeding by American aficionados who are aiming for quality and nobility of carriage as well as for consistent coloring may well end in a new breed whose arresting appearance should ensure its demand on a world-wide scale.

ALBINO

Origin: United States by intent. Other nations usually at random.
Height: Any.
Color: Snow white. Pink skin. Eyes pale blue or dark brown.

Albino is a color as well as being sometimes, though not necessarily always, a breed. If this sounds ambiguous it is because *albino* in a horse, as in any animal, describes a complete absence of pigmentation and as such may occur at random; on the other hand Albino horses tend to breed true to color, and the ability consistently to reproduce given physical character-istics over several generations is the criterion for a breed.

Albino horses have been bred in North America since the early part of this century, all thought to be descended from a prepotent sire named Old King who was a quality saddle horse, possibly of Arab-Morgan origin. They are handsome, lightweight animals with good bone and conformation and kindly, intelligent dispositions. Successes are being achieved in breeding out the weak blue eyes and over-sensitivity of the skin to sun.

AMERICAN QUARTER HORSE

Origin: United States.
Height: 15.2–16.1 hh.
Color: Any solid color, predominantly chestnut.
Character: Intelligent, highly adaptable, sensible and active.
Physique: Short head with wideset, intelligent eyes and open nostrils. Muscular neck well-set on powerful, sloping shoulders; broad, deep chest. Short, muscular back with well-sprung ribs and strong loins. Massive, rounded hindquarters. Clean, hard legs, finer than would be expected on so powerful a body. Short pasterns. The overall effect is that of a compact, muscular horse with elegant legs.

The Quarter Horse is the oldest of the American breeds. It was developed in Virginia and the Carolinas from Arabs, Barbs and Turks brought by the

Palomino

Albino

Spanish and crossed during the early part of the 17th century with imported English animals. The purpose behind this careful selective breeding was the popular colonial sport of match racing, short sprints which usually took place over distances not exceeding a quarter of a mile and were frequently run in the village street. The new breed's superlative performances at the quarter mile earned it the name of Quarter Horse.

The breed is said to possess a natural sense for cows. During the pioneer days it traveled west with the new settlers, excelling at every sort of work with cattle, and was acclaimed by ranchers as the most able and the most intelligent cow horse known to man. Today it is widely used in rodeos. It can spin on a dime, go from a standing start into a gallop, and use its head, and as such it is without peer in these contests.

It is just possibly the most versatile horse in the world. It is certainly the most popular, if numbers can be relied upon for proof. More than 800,000 American Quarter Horses are registered in the United States and abroad, and more than 40 different nations own specimens of the breed. The American Quarter Horse Association in Amarillo, Texas, needs to employ more than 200 people to handle their business, which includes the largest equine registry in the world.

The popularity of the Quarter Horse as a show ring animal unfortunately predisposes it to structural difficulties. As with all show animals, there is a temptation for breeders of the Quarter Horse to produce exaggerated qualities of the breed for display before the judges. The Quarter Horse's heavy shoulders and hindquarters together with his very fine legs and short pasterns needs little refinement to produce a tendency to navicular disease, a chronic form of lameness for which no cure has yet been found.

A new enthusiasm for sprint racing has reestablished the Quarter Horse in his early colonial role. Following his flamboyant successes in an extraordinary number of diverse occupations, it is deeply satisfying that he can now crown his triumphs with the richest prize in racing – the All American Futurity Stakes, worth roughly $600,000.

PINTO

Origin: United States.
Height: Varies.
Color: Black and white in bold patches all over the body (called *overo*, the equivalent of piebald in Great Britain), or white and any other color except black (white and cream, white and brown, etc., called *tobiano*, equivalent of the British skewbald).

The Pinto, or Paint, horse is traditionally associated with American Indians. It is a color breed derived from inherited spotting genes, and there are no precise standards of conformation for it.

American Quarter Horse

Pinto

MORGAN

Origin: United States.
Height: 14–15.2hh.
Color: Bay, brown, black, chestnut.
Character: Kind, independent, active, hard-working and enduring.
Physique: Short, broad head with intelligent eye, set on a thick, muscled neck. Strong shoulder, deep, broad chest, compact, muscular body with strong loins and hindquarters. Good legs with plenty of bone. Abundant mane and tail. Action high and free. A tough, hardy horse with enormous physical strength and endurance.

Few breeds of horse can claim descent from one common foundation sire, but Justin Morgan, foaled about 1793 in Massachusetts, was a stallion of such astonishing prepotency that his stamp in conformation, character and height was reproduced in his offspring so often and so faithfully that a new breed of horse began. It was named for him; or rather for his second owner, since the horse was originally named "Figure" and the later appellation "Justin Morgan" seems to have been an abbreviation of "Justin Morgan's horse." Justin Morgan appears to have changed hands several times, doing gruelling work as a farm horse, winning weight-pulling contests, and also racing unbeaten both in harness and under saddle. He died in Vermont in 1821.

Despite exhaustive research, the parentage of Justin Morgan remains obscure. It seems quite likely that he may have been almost pure Welsh Cob, but claims are also made that he was sired by a Thoroughbred race-horse named True Briton or by a Dutch stallion. The Welsh Cob theory has some support in the preponderance of Welsh family names in the region in which Justin Morgan lived, and has great support in the appearance of the Morgan horse today.

The modern Morgan horse is a taller and more refined version of Justin Morgan. It is an all-purpose breed, popular in harness and under saddle, and its good nature, economy and endurance have made it deservedly popular.

TENNESSEE WALKING HORSE

Origin: United States.
Height: 15–16hh.
Color: All solid colors.
Character: Docile, kind, willing and gay.
Physique: Plain head with prick ears, nobly carried on a strong, arched neck. Strong, sloping shoulder with broad chest. Broad, powerful body with strong loins and hindquarters. Clean, hard legs. Abundant mane and tail, usually worn long and full, and artificially high tail carriage.

Like the Morgan, the Tennessee Walking Horse traces to one prepotent

Morgan

Tennessee Walking Horse

stallion, a Standardbred trotter named Black Allan, who was foaled in 1886. Black Allan contained both Morgan and Hambletonian blood. Other breeds who contributed to the Tennessee Walker were the Thoroughbred, Saddlebred, and Narragansett Pacer. The Walker was developed through selective breeding by southern plantation owners who aimed for a combination of stamina with great comfort and smoothness of gait.

The results have been extremely successful. The Tennessee Walker has acquired a unique running walk gait which makes it about the most comfortable ride in the world. It is a gait that apparently cannot be taught to any other breed, but in the Tennessee Walker it is now almost inbred, so that foals are sometimes seen to perform it without any other instruction but that of imitating their dams. The action of the forefeet is high and straight; that of the hind feet very long-striding. The horse moves with a four-beat gait, the forefoot touching the ground fractionally before the diagonally opposite hind foot, which oversteps the track of the forefoot by some 6–15in. The effect is that of a steady, gentle, gliding movement, and the horse swings into his own rhythm with a nodding head and clicking teeth.

AMERICAN SADDLEBRED (KENTUCKY SADDLER)

Origin: United States.
Height: 15–16hh.
Color: Black, brown, bay, gray, chestnut. White markings usual.
Character: Superb riding horse with great presence and a gentle, charming nature.
Physique: Small, alert head, with straight face, alert eye, open nostrils, prick ears, gaily carried on an arched neck. Strong shoulders, body short, muscled and well ribbed up, strong, flexible hindquarters. Hard legs with supple joints and flexible pasterns. Neat, round feet. Full mane and tail. The tail is carried exaggeratedly high – usually an artificial tail carriage, created by nicking the muscles of the dock and setting in a crupper. Action extravagant, collected and precise; tremendously showy.

The five gaits of the American Saddle Horse are the walk, trot, canter, slow gait and rack. The rack is an even four-beat gait in which each foot pauses in mid air before coming down separately – a spectacular, prancing gait which can occur at speeds up to 30mph. The slow gait is a slow and graceful version of the rack.

Even at the walk, trot and canter, these horses have the grace of ballet dancers. They were developed, like the slightly-heavier Tennessee Walker, from a mixture of Thoroughbred, Morgan and Narragensett Pacer stock, and, also like the Tennessee Walker, their original purpose was to provide plantation owners with a luxury ride. Nowadays they are usually bred for the show ring, where they compete in separate classes for three-gaited (walk, trot and canter only) and five-gaited horses according to their level of education.

American Saddlebred (Kentucky Saddler)

AMERICAN STANDARDBRED

Origin: United States.
Height: Around 15.2hh.
Color: Any solid color; usually black, bay, brown, chestnut.
Character: Courageous and very game.
Physique: Conformation varies somewhat, since the prime requirement of a Standardbred is its speed and not its pretty face. It is a small, muscular Thoroughbred type, longer in the body and shorter in the leg and of less refined appearance. It has powerful shoulders, deep, broad chest and strong hindquarters. Legs and feet are iron hard. It has immense stamina and splendid heart and lungs.

The name "Standardbred" applies to both trotters and pacers, and comes from a 1-mile speed trial standard requirement for entry in races. Entrants must attain standards of 2 minutes 30 seconds for trotters and 2 minutes 25 seconds for pacers. Pacing is a gait in which both legs on the same side come down simultaneously.

The Standardbred, although predominantly Thoroughbred, also contains a mixture of English and Canadian trotting and Hackney blood together with Arab, Barb and Morgan. The breed descends from Hambletonian

10, foaled in 1849 and the sire of 1,321 offspring, and through him from the English Thoroughbred Messenger, imported in 1788.

Harness racing is one of the most popular of American sports, and Standardbred breeding has become big business.

HACKNEY HORSE

Origin: England.
Height: Usually 14.3–15.3hh (Great Britain); 14.2–16hh (USA). Can be taller.
Color: Black, bay, brown, chestnut, occasionally roan.
Character: Alert, vigorous and full of life and spirit.
Physique: Neat head with straight face, large, intelligent eye, short prick ears, carried high and proud on an arched, muscled neck; strong shoulders with prominent withers, well-sprung ribs and muscular, rounded hindquarters. Strong, straight legs with flexible joints and short pasterns; neat, round, hard feet, rather small. Tail set on high and carried high – in the United States the muscles of the dock are often nicked to induce an artificially high carriage.

The Hackney is distinguished by its proud and graceful carriage and by its attractively flamboyant paces. Even at a standstill it holds itself with great presence; at a walk it moves with a springing, airy step, and at a trot the forelegs are drawn up high with sharply-bent knee and thrown well forward with a ground-covering stride while the hindlegs move in a similar exaggerated action, being propelled well forward under the body. The action should be straight and true, with a tiny pause of each foot in mid air which almost makes it appear to float.

(For more information see Hackney Pony, page 100.)

IRISH COB

Origin: Ireland.
Height: 15–16hh.
Color: Any. Black, bay, chestnut and gray are the most common.
Character: Sensible, active. A hard worker with endurance.
Physique: Plain head with convex face, strong neck set on powerful shoulders, strong, sturdy body and hindquarters. Legs short and iron hard with plenty of bone, feet large and round and dense.

This extremely strong and capable harness horse, still questionable as a definite breed although the type has existed in Ireland for centuries, is now unfortunately declining in numbers through being made redundant by motorization. It had its heyday in the 18th and 19th centuries, being the sort of horse which could be trusted to take a loaded cart to market or pull a milk float all day without tiring or becoming impatient. It still enjoys success as a sensible hack for a heavy rider. (Illustrated on page 127.)

American Standardbred

Hackney Horse

IRISH DRAUGHT HORSE

Origin: Ireland.
Height: 15–17hh.
Color: Bay, brown, chestnut, gray.
Character: Quiet, sensible, willing and active.
Physique: Alert head with straight face, carried well on short, strong neck. Body barrel-shaped and rather long, with massive shoulders and powerful, sloping quarters. Legs very hard, showing abundant bone and having only a little feather on the heels. Feet large and round.

This horse, when crossed with a Thoroughbred or other quality lightweight horse, gives rise to the famous Irish hunters and jumpers. It could be argued that it belongs in the "cold blood" section of this book, but the absence of feather on its heels and the general alert air of the riding horse makes its categorization at least questionable.

IRISH HUNTER

Origin: Ireland.
Height: Usually 16–16.3hh.
Color: Any solid color.
Character: Intelligent, bold, sensible, enduring.
Physique: Handsome animal of classic hunting and showjumping type, having an alert head of Thoroughbred appearance, excellent shoulder and heart room, strong, sloping quarters, hard legs with ample bone, and good feet.

Both as hunter and showjumper the Irish horse – even today a type rather than a breed – is internationally acclaimed. (See also Hunter, page 219.)

CLEVELAND BAY

Origin: England.
Height: 15.2–16.1hh.
Color: Bay or bay brown. White markings not desirable, but a small star or white hairs showing in the heels is acceptable.
Character: Intelligent, active, sensible, calm, and of bottomless endurance.
Physique: Large head with convex profile and kind eye. Longish neck on good shoulder. A rather long body, deep-girthed and roomy round heart. Powerful hindquarters, with tail set on fairly high. Legs short and hard with excellent bone and good feet.

The Cleveland Bay is one of the oldest, if not actually the oldest, of the established English breeds. In earlier times it was known as the Chapman Horse, named for the chapmen, or traveling merchants, who used it as a packhorse in the 17th and 18th centuries. Improvement with Thoroughbred

Irish Cob

Irish Draught Horse

blood in the late 18th century led to the sideshoot of the Cleveland Bay, the now nearly-extinct Yorkshire Coach Horse, which was a taller and flashier version of the Cleveland model.

Today, with a dash of Thoroughbred blood added over the last two centuries, the Cleveland Bay is in worldwide demand as a ceremonial coach horse. It is also much sought after for crossing with Thoroughbreds to produce ideal hunter types.

THOROUGHBRED

Origin: England.
Height: Averagely around, or just over, 16hh. It is possible to get them as small as 14.2hh or as large as 17.3hh according to the purpose for which they are bred. Hacks are usually 14.2–15.3hh, sprinters 15.1–16.1hh, stayers and steeplechasers 15.2–16.3hh, and hunters 15.1–17.3hh.
Color: Black, brown, bay, chestnut, gray.
Character: Bold, active and brave.
Physique: Varies slightly according to type, hacks being comparatively light-framed, sprinters having muscled, compact bodies, 'chasers usually big-framed with generous bone. Head aristocratic, with straight face, large, intelligent eye; neck long and proudly arched, set into good, sloping shoulders and deep chest. Prominent withers, short, strong back with deep girth and well-sprung ribs. Hindquarters generous and well-muscled, and can be either sloping or flat. Excellent legs showing good bone, short cannon bones, springy pasterns. Round feet, tending to be brittle. Coat fine and silky, showing small veins underneath the skin, and mane and tail fine and smooth. Action free, long-striding, and very fast.

The Thoroughbred is probably the only breed to be better known by the name of his usual trade: the racehorse. His emergence as a breed begins as recently as the early 18th century – at a time when racing had been known to exist for at least 5,000 years. The beginnings of racing are so far back that they are beyond recorded history, though there are instructions for training racehorses on Hittite cuneiform tablets dated about 3,200 BC. The Chinese, Greeks and Romans are known to have enjoyed racing, but it was probably not until the Roman occupation of Britain that racing was introduced to England, the birthplace of the racehorse.

For more than 1,000 years following the Roman occupation races took place in a limited way all over Britain. They were usually held on public holidays, in market places or as private matches arranged between gentlemen, and it was not until the early 17th century, during the reign of King James I, that racing began to have any organization. James built a palace at Newmarket, a tiny East Anglian village that was to become the center of British racing, and visited with his Court for sporting holidays. Though he preferred hunting and hawking to racing, racing was very popular in Scotland at the time and Scottish members of the Court soon established the sport at Newmarket. James recognized the military and civil importance

Cleveland Bay

Thoroughbred

of improving the speed and stamina of British horses and encouraged the importation of good foreign horses to strengthen the breed.

Racing survived at Newmarket under Charles I, who was not a great racing man, and blossomed under Charles II, who could not have been keener. Charles II founded races at Newmarket known as Royal Plates, and liked to come and watch the racing every summer, with Nell Gwynn kept more or less discreetly down the road. He is the only English king to have won a race on the flat with himself as jockey, and one of the Newmarket courses existing today, the Rowley Mile, is named for his favorite hack, Old Rowley.

With such royal patronage the popularity of racing increased. By this time (mid-17th century) a better class of racehorse was evolving, bred from the fastest native mares crossed with imported stallions which were usually Arabs, Barbs or Turks. This early stock had not the exceptional turn of foot of the modern racehorse, which is taller and therefore has a longer stride; nor were its bloodlines yet sufficiently established for it to be described as a breed.

The three foundation sires from which all Thoroughbreds trace arrived in England a half century later. They were the Darley Arabian, who was sent to England in 1704 by Thomas Darley, the British Consul in Aleppo; the Byerley Turk, who was Colonel Byerley's battle horse; and the Godolphin Arabian, probably part of a gift of horses to the King of France from the Bey of Tunis and later acquired from the shafts of a Paris milk float for Lord Godolphin's stud at Cambridge. These three were bred onto the best of the English racing mares with such success that today no Thoroughbred registered in the General Stud Book does not have one or all of them in his pedigree (in some cases they reoccur many thousands of times).

At this time racing was still the hobby of the rich and aristocratic, and another hundred years and more were to pass before the Thoroughbred racehorse began to emerge as the foundation of a colossal industry. Somewhere around 1752 the Jockey Club, later to become the governing body of British racing, began as a social club for racing and horsebreeding gentlemen, and its most influential early member was Sir Charles Bunbury, who, with the Earl of Derby, was the founder of the Epsom Derby – the race that was to become the greatest all-round test of a three-year-old in the world. It might have been called the Bunbury but for the toss of a coin. Lord Derby won the call but Bunbury won the first Derby (1780) with his colt Diomed.

Half a century later the Derby was established as the race of the year and race meetings were no longer only for the wealthy. The coming of the railways no longer meant that horses and spectators had to live within walking distance of Epsom.

The Derby was a great event in Victorian times. For much of the country it was a public holiday: even Parliament did not sit on Derby Day. Massive crowds thronged to the racecourse and side-shows, fairs and other amusements added to the entertainment. Scandals, frauds and doping abounded.

One of the coolest villains of the Turf was Francis Ignatius Coyle, who

Thoroughbred Racing

played a daring part in the Great Swindle of 1844. The Derby of that year was won by a horse entered as Running Rein, which was recognized by an Irish farmer as a four-year-old named Maccabaeus. An objection was lodged, and Running Rein's owner (presumably not part of the plot) brought an action for the recovery of the prize money. The all-important piece of evidence was the horse, and a judge's order was issued for the training yard where it was stabled to be kept under close surveillance by detectives so that the horse could not be removed.

A day was quickly set for several veterinary surgeons to examine Running Rein to establish his age beyond doubt. Early on the morning of this critical day Ignatius Coyle, who had business with Running Rein's trainer, rode into the stable yard on his hack. When his business had been concluded he remounted his hack and rode quietly away through the cordon of detectives. The "hack" he rode away on was Running Rein. The horse was never seen again.

Meanwhile foreign interest in the Thoroughbred was beginning to develop. The French, who were to become perhaps the finest breeders of staying racehorses in the world, took the English triple crown (Two Thousand Guineas, Derby and St Leger) in 1865 with Gladiateur, who they nicknamed "the Avenger of Waterloo". The first American victory in the Derby happened in 1881 with Iroquois. In 1897 the great American jockey Tod Sloan arrived in England. Until that time, English jockeys had raced with long stirrups, often using spurs, and races tended to be leisurely, with an accelerated pace over the last two furlongs. Sloan's style was different. Crouching low with short stirrups and short reins, getting off to a fast start and winning his races from in front, he was at first ridiculed by the English. But his style proved to be extremely effective. English jockeys soon learned to adapt to it and have ridden short ever since. Although Sloan never won the Derby, compatriots of his who rode in the same fashion won 4 of the first 12 Derbies of the 20th century.

Early in the 20th century Italy, thanks mainly to one man, Federico Tesio, built up a stud which was to produce such great horses as Nearco, Donatello II and Ribot, who have had enormous world-wide influence. Representatives of some 50 other nations began to appear at English racehorse auctions, and for the best part of half a century Britain did an enormous trade in Thoroughbred export.

Today it declines. Through lack of foresight, lack of money, and lack of encouragement to the best owners and breeders to operate in the British Isles much of the cream of the English Thoroughbred has been skimmed off abroad. Hyperion's progeny (Derby winner 1933) in America in tail male has won more than $40,000,000. Vaguely Noble, outstanding two-year-old of 1967, was sold to America for the then record price of 136,000 guineas, went on to win Europe's richest prize, the French Prix de l'Arc de Triomphe, was syndicated for $6,000,000 and is today siring some of America's most brilliant stock. In the years 1968–72 four of the five English Derby winners were bred in North America.

The modern American racing industry is the richest in the world and beyond question produces the most precocious and brilliant young Thoroughbreds of any nation, while the French have a deservedly high reputation for older middle-distance horses and stayers. (France has a brilliant incentive scheme for breeders, on condition the horse is both foaled and raced in France.) But of all the racehorse-breeding nations Ireland seems to be the most stable, plucking young steeplechasers of consistent excellence from farmyard, barn and hunting field.

No matter how it is dispersed, the Thoroughbred still commands the highest prices and is the biggest industry by far of all horse breeds. It is the fastest horse in the world. It is also one of the finest riding horses, excelling in the hunting field, the show ring, at three-day eventing, and as an elegant and spirited hack.

ARAB

Origin: Arabia. Now widespread throughout the world, many countries having produced separate strains.
Height: Roughly 14.2–15.1hh, but can be smaller and occasionally a trifle larger according to severity of climate and richness of pasture.
Color: Gray, bay, chestnut; occasionally black.
Character: Remarkably spirited horse, fiery and airy; possessed of great intelligence; bold, loyal, and enduring.

Physique: Exquisite head, short and fine, with concave face, wide nostrils on an elegant muzzle, large, dark eyes and small, prick ears; carried nobly on a graceful arched neck, set into good shoulders. Body compact and well-muscled with strong hindquarters; legs at once delicate and strong; feet small and hard. The whole effect is one of symmetry and grace, carried with pride and full of life, and the action straight, free and airy.

Allah said to the South Wind: "Become solid flesh, for I will make a new creature of thee, to the honour of My Holy One, and the abasement of Mine enemies, and for a servant to them that are subject to Me."

And the South Wind said: "Lord, do Thou so."

Then Allah took a handful of the South Wind and he breathed thereon, creating the horse and saying: "Thy name shall be Arabian, and virtue bound into the hair of thy forelock, and plunder on thy back. I have preferred thee above all beasts of burden, inasmuch as I have made thee master thy friend. I have given thee the power of flight without wings, be it in onslaught or in retreat, I will set men on thy back, that shall honor and praise Me and sing Hallelujah to My name." Bedouin legend.

The Arab horse has been selectively bred for more than 1,000 years longer than any other breed, and there are those who claim that he has run wild in the deserts of Arabia for many millennia. Others disagree on the

Arab

grounds that no prehistoric horse bones have ever been found in the desert, and they are supported by the fact that the Arab was not one of the 12 breeds mentioned by the Romans; nor is there any mention of him in pre-Roman history. The Mohammedans believed, literally, that Allah created him out of a handful of the south wind; but the mundane truth of it must be that, like all other breeds of horse and pony, the Arab evolved over many centuries from the prehistoric wild horses who roamed the plateaux and steppes of Europe and Asia before man was civilized, and who looked very much like the Tarpan and the Asiatic Wild Horse of today.

Selective breeding of the Arab by the Bedouin has been going on since at least the time of Mohammed (7th century AD), and there is evidence to suggest that it was practised for as long as a thousand years before that. The Bedouins' ruthless attention to purity of line — so absolute that unless a horse was known to be *asil* (pure) he could never be bred into the *asil* line, no matter how perfect his conformation — plus the exceptional hardships of the desert climate are the two factors that have produced this, the most graceful and individual horse in the world. Food was scarce in the desert. Grass grew only in winter and early spring, and for the rest of the year the horses lived off camel's milk, dried dates, locusts, and dried camel's meat. Only the strong could endure it. So convinced was Mohammed of the military importance of these tough desert horses, which he bought from the wandering tribes and paid for with human slaves, that he wrote into the Koran an irresistable injunction to men to feed their horses well: "As many grains of barley as thou givest thy horse, so many sins shall be forgiven thee."

Religious commandment reinforced by an extraordinary passion for their horses led the Bedouin into a man-to-horse relationship unequalled to this day. It was to last for 13 centuries. Not only did a man share his food with his horse, but even slept with him; and this, too, was on the instruction of Mohammed ("The Evil One dare not enter into a tent in which a pure-bred horse is kept"). The mares, and not the stallions, were the most highly prized and were the mounts that were used for war and plunder. Purity of blood line was treated with fanatical seriousness, and horses were generally inbred to reinforce good qualities — an entirely foreign concept to the Western breeder, whose school of thought has it that inbreeding produces congenital weaknesses. The several hundred "families" of the Arabian horse divided into three main types, which are still to be seen today. They are:

Kehylan — masculine type, symbol of power and endurance,

Seglawi — feminine type, symbol of beauty and elegance,

Muniqi — angular type, symbol of speed and racing.

The breeding of one Arabian type with another is not always desirable, since the offspring is sometimes of lesser quality than either parent.

Arabs were probably first introduced into Europe during the Moorish invasions of the western Mediterranean. Incidental breeding with local mares must have occurred, but there is little evidence to suggest that the Arab was thought of as anything more than perhaps a decorative parade

Head of Krisoon Arab

Head of Uracur Arab

Head of Shammar Arab

Head of Taraszczra Arab

mount. During the Crusades, captured Arab horses seem again to have acquired some stature as fit mounts for kings and princes on state occasions, though as cavalry chargers they never entered into consideration because the heavy armor of the times required horses of enormous size and power to carry it. Light arms and armor changed all that. From the Renaissance through the Napoleonic wars the superiority of the Turkish mounts, in fleetness of foot and movement and in endurance, was obvious, and the demand for Arab blood began to grow in Europe. Following the disastrous retreat from Moscow in the bitter winter of 1812, Napoleon's aide-de-camp wrote to his superior officer:

The Arab horse withstood the exertions and privations better than the European horse. After the cruel campaign in Russia almost all the horses the Emperor had left were his Arabs. General Hubert . . . was only able to bring back to France one horse out of his five, and that was an Arab. Captain Simonneau, of the General Staff, had only his Arab left at the end, and so it was with me also.

Given such proofs as these, Arabians were wanted wherever courage and stamina were at a premium and so it came about that during the Crimean War vital news of the Russian defeat was entrusted to an Arab-mounted messenger. The bay stallion Omar Pasha galloped the 93 miles from Silistra to Varna in one day. His rider died of exhaustion, but Omar Pasha seemed fresh as ever . . . Arab horses are sometimes known as Drinkers of the Wind.

Today the Arabian is bred in many countries, showing slight differences of type according to national preference and variations in height and build according to the climate and the pasture (obviously a horse bred on rich temperate-zone pasture will be bigger and softer than his dry, desert-bred cousin). Though his cavalry days are over, his dash and spirit as a riding horse ensure his future and his prepotency as a sire will endure, as in so many cases in the past, wherever a new breed of quality and fire is evolved.

ANGLO-ARAB

Origin: Evolved in several countries by interbreeding Thoroughbreds with Arabs. Principal countries of Anglo-Arab development are Britain, France and Poland.
Height: Usually around 16hh, or just under, but can be smaller or larger.
Color: Any of the common solid colors. Bay and chestnut are the most usual.
Character: Brave, gay, sweet-natured, intelligent.
Physique: Varies; the qualities of Thoroughbred and Arab being displayed in differing measure. An elegant lightweight saddle horse with delicate head, usually a straight face, and large, expressive eyes. Neck long and arched. Prominent withers, good shoulder and chest, pleasing depth of girth. Short back; tail set on high and gaily carried. Legs long and slender, with good quality bone.

The Anglo-Arab, obviously a younger breed than the Thoroughbred, arose independently in various parts of Europe wherever there were breeders who admired the Thoroughbred and the Arab and wanted to combine the qualities of both. Studs in south-western France and the Polish government stud at Janów produce particularly good Anglo-Arabs.

Depending on individual height and scope, Anglo-Arabs have excelled at dressage, eventing, jumping, hunting and as hacks.

SHAGYA ARAB

Origin: Hungary.
Height: Roughly 15hh.
Color: Gray (almost always).
Character: Extremely versatile, alert, intelligent, and enduring.
Physique: Typical Arabian of the Seglawi type.

The Shagya is not a purebred Arab in the strictest sense, since some of the early foundation mares were not Arabian. It has its origins at the Bábolna stud, where in 1816 an army order was issued that all Bábolna mares should be covered by Oriental stallions. During the 1830s, following a catastrophic outbreak of venereal disease at the stud, the Bábolna commandant, Major Freiherr von Herbert, imported from the desert 5 Arab mares and 9 stallions, the best of which, a gray called Shagya, was to prove a sire of great pre-potency.

The descendants of Shagya are now at stud in the United States, Poland, Germany, Austria, Rumania, Yugoslavia and Czechoslovakia, and are still bred at Bábolna. Stallions take the name Shagya followed by a Roman numeral indicating the number of generations separating them from the foundation sire.

Shagyas have been used for all kinds of work. Though they are primarily cavalry and general saddle horses they have worked successfully as draught animals and go well in harness.

TERSKY

Origin: USSR – Stavropol region.
Height: Average 15hh.
Color: Gray.
Character: Kind, intelligent, enduring.
Physique: Three types exist, the light, medium, and thickset. Elegant, medium-sized head with straight face, large, liquid eye and longish, pricked ears. Long, well-carried neck set on good shoulders; prominent withers, a longish back with strong loins, good hindquarters with high-set tail. Legs fine, and with good bone.

Founded on the remnants of the old Streletsk Arab, which was in fact an Anglo-Arab with predominant Arab blood, mixed with Kabardin, Don, and

Anglo-Arab

Shagya Arab

Thoroughbred blood, and reinforced with more Arabian, the Tersky began to take shape in 1925 and was officially recognized in 1948. It was evolved on the State stud at Tersk in the northern Caucasus, and the aim behind its breeding was to produce a horse with the Arab qualities of air and endurance, a hardy sort who would make a good steeplechaser.

The modern Tersky is in fact used as a flat-race horse, competing not against Thoroughbreds (it hasn't the speed) but against Arabians. It is an excellent cross country and dressage mount, and its beauty and versatility have created some demand for it as a circus horse.

HISPANO (SPANISH ANGLO-ARAB)

Origin: Spain — Estremadura and Andalusia.
Height: Around 16hh.
Color: Usually bay, chestnut, gray.
Character: Brave, intelligent, handy. An excellent and versatile saddle horse.
Physique: See Anglo-Arab.

The Hispano is a Spanish Anglo-Arab based on Spanish Arabian mares crossed with English Thoroughbred stallions. It is a splendid all-round saddle horse for any skilled performance, and is popular for eventing, jumping, hunting and dressage as well as being the preferred mount of the military for sporting competitions.

Because of its bravery and quick ability on its feet it is also used for testing the courage of young bulls. This is done by the rider pushing the bullock over with a pole to see whether he will stand up again and charge, and obviously requires a nimble mount of spirit and quick brain.

PLEVEN

Origin: Bulgaria.
Height: About 15.2hh.
Color: Bright chestnut.
Character: Kind, intelligent, brave, spirited.
Physique: Robust Anglo-Arab horse with a fiery Arab look about it. Very handsome. Excellent conformation.

The Pleven originated at the turn of the century on the State agricultural farm of Georgi Dimitrov near Pleven, Bulgaria. The mixed breeding that produced it started with Russian Anglo-Arabs bred onto local Arabian and cross-bred mares, and continued for a quarter of a century with additions of purebred Arab and Hungarian Gidran (Thoroughbred crossed with native mares) stock. About 1938 the type became fixed, though it has subsequently received careful injections of selected English Thoroughbred blood.

The result is a magnificent all-purpose lightweight horse, a first-rate all round saddle animal which is also sometimes used in agriculture. The

Tersky

Pleven is a natural jumper, good enough to perform in international contests. It is now widely bred throughout Bulgaria.

BARB

Origin: North Africa – Algeria, Morocco.
Height: 14–15hh.
Color: Dark bay, brown, chestnut, black, gray.
Character: An extremely tough horse, able to live on small quantities of poor food. Docile, courageous.
Physique: Long but refined head, with a straight face. Flat shoulders. Sloping quarters with a low-set tail. Long, strong legs.

When he is awakened and rode upon his mettle, no horse is more nimble, vigorous and adroit, and better for an action [battle] of one or two hours. He makes a good stallion to breed running horses [racehorses], the colts that he gets being generally well winded, fleet and good at bottom [stayers].
Richard Blome, *The Gentleman's Recreation, 1686.*

The Barb is one of the great foundation horses which was widely used to strengthen and improve other breeds. As early as AD 800 it was exported in quantity to Spain with the Moorish invasion, where, crossed with the native Spanish horses, it gave rise to the Andalusian (Oriental horses other than Barbs also contributed to the new breed). While the Turks occupied the eastern half of the Mediterranean the Barbary coast was for years open to traders, many of whom took the Barb away with them to wherever home might be and crossed him with their local horses.

In 1662 King Charles II of England married the Barbary port of Tangier (it was part of his wife's dowry). Charles's great passion was racing. In the 21 years of his rule Barbs were exported plentifully to England, where they were used to improve the speed and stamina of early British racehorses and were thus forerunners of the Thoroughbred (not to be recognized as a breed for another half-century). When Tangier passed back to the Moors the exportation of Barbs was so widespread that by the 18th century inferior Barbs could be bought very cheaply in places as distant as northern Europe.

LIBYAN BARB

Origin: Libya.
Height: 14–15hh.
Color: Black, brown, bay, chestnut, gray.
Character: Active, intelligent, frugal and enduring.
Physique: A lightweight saddle horse of varying conformation. Though its bloodlines are aristocratic, it is much used as an everyday working animal and as such it is normally not selectively bred and so is not often anything out of the way to look at.

The Libyan Barb stems from Arab and Barb bloodlines with unspecified additions. It is the common mount of North Africa. It is hardy, has abundant stamina and can do well on poor fare, and has some ability as a sprinter.

ANDALUSIAN

Origin: Spain.
Height: About 16hh.
Color: Nearly always gray. Can be black.
Character: Intelligent, affectionate and proud.
Physique: Medium-big head with slightly convex face, large, expressive eyes, neat ears, carried nobly on a strong, crested neck. Big, well-made shoulder, deep chest. Longish, straight back; broad, compact body with strong loins, powerful, rounded hindquarters. Legs clean and strong, with hocks well let down and short cannon bones.

Spanish historians claim that there were horses in the Iberian peninsula before the subsidence of the Straits of Gibraltar, and that these horses came from Africa. The first importation of horses to Spain on record were the 2,000 Numidean mares brought by Hasdrubel of Carthage – legendary animals who were claimed to be "faster than the wind," and who were left to run wild in Iberia until the Roman invasion of 200 BC. The Romans tamed this Spanish horse, but after their retreat it was free to run wild again.

Barb

Andalusian

Over some 600 years, Spanish horses bred naturally without human selection. The beginnings of a true type came into existence following the invasion by northern European barbarians, mainly Teutonic, who conquered the part of Spain later to be named for them – Vandalusia. The Vandals brought with them horses of a "pure Germanic" type; tall horses, with long slender necks and stout bodies, who interbred with the indigenous Spanish animals.

In 711 AD the Moslems invaded Spain and stayed for eight centuries. In the first wave of the invasion they brought with them 300,000 horses which were almost certainly Barbs. The first official stud, at Cordoba, was started by the Moslem Almanzor, and the Barb-Teutonic-Iberian cross began to stabilize into the Spanish horse.

Fighting the Moslems taught the Spanish to breed for selective purposes. Riding the heavyweight German-Spanish type of horse they had little chance against the fantastic agility of the Arab- and Barb-mounted Moslems, who could dart in from the side and, with the use of razor-sharp stirrups, slash the Spanish horses' tendons simply by sticking out a leg. About the time of the conquest of Granada (11th century) the Catholic kings switched over to light cavalry, heavy armor was abandoned, and the Spanish horse became not just a means of transport but a fighting animal. This was achieved by mixing the Spanish horse freely with Oriental blood. From this time onwards Spanish horses of the Andalusian type spread throughout Europe, where they contributed enormously to the improvement of native stock.

The military importance of good horses had been thoroughly impressed upon the Spanish leaders, and throughout the Middle Ages the kings of Spain practised selective breeding and offered inducements to breeders – large-scale breeders could not be imprisoned for debt, their eldest sons were exempt from military service, and so on. In 1571 Philip II founded the first Royal Stud at Cordoba and opened the first stud book.

The greatest breeders of the true Andalusian were undoubtedly the monks, whose obsession with purity of line was little short of the fanatical, and who even threatened to excommunicate followers who veered away from the national equestrian style. In 1476 the Carthusian monks in Jerez acquired 10,000 acres of land through a bequest, and, along with two other Carthusian monasteries, began the production of Andalusians, bringing to the job an intelligence and devotion that was greatly aided by the enormous wealth of the Church at their disposal.

It was as well that the Carthusian interest had been aroused, since Andalusians had a disastrous time at the Royal Stud during the reign of Philip III. Hieronymo Tiuti, manager of the stud, crossed the purebreds in his charge indiscriminately with Norman, Danish and Neapolitan stallions, all of which were Roman-nosed, producing a slower, heavier type of carriage horse. Later, Napoleon's marshals creamed off the best of the Spanish studs and wiped out many of the divergent strains. No good Andalusians were left, save for a few concealed here and there by the Carthusians and a small herd hidden by the Zapata family.

In the 19th century a new stud was begun under Ferdinand VII and the

Andalusian began to prosper once again. Despite religious persecution the Carthusian monks persevered with their own line of Andalusian selection, which has resulted in a very slightly coarser type of horse known as the Andalusian-Carthusian, or Carthusian.

LIPIZZANER

Origin: Austria.
Height: 15–16hh.
Color: Predominantly gray. Sometimes bay, chestnut, roan.
Character: Excellent – intelligent, willing, obedient and sweet-natured.
Physique: As Andalusian, though face is often straight. The Lipizzaner is slightly smaller than the Andalusian, and carries itself with possibly even greater presence.

The Lipizzaner is the mount of the famous Spanish Riding School of Vienna, founded in 1758 "for the education of the nobility in the art of horsemanship." Only stallions are used in the School, and years of patient training lie behind the performances of the advanced high school Airs for which the White Horses of Vienna are world-renowned. The stallion in the illustration is executing the *capriole* (see also page 18).

Lipizzaner

The Lipizzaner has been bred in Austria since the 16th century, the foundation stud being at Lipizza, from which the horse takes its name. The original Lipizza stock was pure Andalusian. At Piber, another famous Austrian stud, Andalusians were mixed with Kladrubers, Neapolitans (an important Italian breed of Andalusian mixed with a little Barb and Arab, now extinct), and probably a dash of Fredriksborg and Arab. Bloodlines belonging to Lipizza, Piber and Kladruby were frequently blended. The result, both in the Lipizzaner and the Kladruber, is a horse of predominantly Andalusian origin and great similarity of appearance.

KLADRUBER

Origin: Czechoslovakia.
Height: 16–17.2hh.
Color: Gray; occasionally black.
Character and Physique: Taller, but otherwise almost identical, version of the Andalusian/Lipizzaner, with a convex face. Superb carriage horse personality, being proud, obedient, intelligent and good-natured.

During the 16th century the Emperor Maximilian II founded a stud of Andalusian horses at Kladruby in Bohemia. There, Kladrubers, as they came to be called, were bred with great purity of line; the only new blood, it seems, coming from exchanges with other imperial studs of the Austro-Hungarian empire such as those at Lipizza and Piber, which anyway stocked horses of almost exclusively Andalusian origin.

Today the Kladruber is still bred at the State stud at Kladruby, performing its ancestral function of drawing the State coach on ceremonial occasions. The famous Kladruby Grays are driven in teams of up to 16-in-hand, usually without postillions to assist the coachman.

ALTER-REAL

Origin: Portugal.
Height: 15–16hh.
Color: Bay, brown, occasionally gray.
Character: Intelligent and highly-strung, brave and temperamental. With careful handling it makes a brilliant saddle horse, willing and obedient to the disciplines of haute école.
Physique: Medium-sized head with wide-set, liquid eyes, well-carried on a crested neck. Shoulder strong and muscular with deep chest; body short, powerful and compact, with strong loins and good hindquarters. Hard legs with good bone, fine in the cannon and shannon bones and in the pasterns, with strong forearms and flexible hocks. Has much the look of the Andalusian, and is a saddle horse of great quality.

This famous Portuguese breed originates from 300 of the finest Andalusian mares who were bought by the House of Braganza in 1747 to found a National Stud at Vila de Portel in Alentejo Province.

Kladruber

Alter-Real

During the 18th century the Altér was used by the royal manège in the same advanced classical equitation that was concurrently popular with the Spanish Riding School of Vienna. But the breed was decimated by Napoleon, disastrously outcrossed to foreign breeds such as the Arab, Thoroughbred, Norman and Hanoverian, and it was not until a century later that the Altér was restored by the introduction of Andalusian animals from the Zapata herd (see Andalusian, page 144). Intelligent management by the Ministry of Economy in 1932 brought about the great quality of the modern breed by breeding only from a selected few of the very best Altérs.

LUSITANO

Origin: Portugal.
Height: 15–16hh.
Color: Usually gray, but can be any solid color.
Character: Intelligent, responsive, obedient and exceptionally brave.
Physique: Medium-small head with straight face, small ears and alert expression. Muscular neck on excellent shoulder. Compact body with deep girth and strong loins, rounded hindquarters. Long, fine legs. Mane and tail inclined to be wavy. Handsome sort, recognizably akin to Andalusian.

The Lusitano's background is obscure. The breed has existed in Portugal for several centuries, and is probably of basic Andalusian stock with perhaps some extra Arabian thrown in.

Once a cavalry horse, it is now much used in the bull ring. Mounted bullfighters, called *rejoneadores*, perform entirely from the horse and train their mounts to exacting standards of haute école. It is considered a disgrace for the horse ever to be touched by the bull.

FRENCH SADDLE HORSE (SELLE FRANÇAIS), ANGLO-NORMAN, NORMAN

Origin: France.
Height: 15.2–16.3hh.
Color: Usually chestnut or bay, but can be any color.
Character: Brave, calm, good-tempered.
Physique: Strong saddle horse of hunter type. Head broad with wide-set eyes, tapering to a comparatively narrow muzzle. Ears long and alert. Long strong neck well set into powerful, sloping shoulders. Good, roomy chest and deep girth. Back fairly long and well-ribbed-up. Muscular hindquarters. Legs long, with excellent bone and hocks well let down.

It would be wrong to suggest that the Norman, the Anglo-Norman and the French Saddle Horse are one and the same. They are included under one heading because they are all developments on the same theme, with no precisely-defined point marking a transition from one sort to another. To confuse the issue, there are two very different types of horse both bearing

Lusitano

French Saddle Horse (Selle Français), Anglo-Norman

the name Norman, one a lightweight saddle horse and the other a cob so strong and stocky that it would be more appropriately listed under the heading of "Cold-Blood". To dispense with the Norman Cob, it is a muscular draught animal of good conformation, standing about 16hh; an active horse with a free, high action, a good disposition, and lots of stamina. Hereinafter the name Norman should be taken to apply to the saddle type, except where otherwise specified.

As long as 1,000 years ago there appears to have existed in France a good, solid, spirited animal of the heavy draught type called the Norman horse. William the Conqueror is said to have brought it to England as a war horse. Quite possibly this was the famous Great Horse from which the British heavy draught breeds are descended. Its decline through the Middle Ages, especially during the time when maneuverability took precedence over heavy armor and the draught breeds lost their value as military mounts, is obscure, but during the 16th and 17th centuries the Norman horse emerges again as a useful, rather common, working animal.

In the 17th century, importations of German and Scandinavian stallions, also Arabs and Barbs to a lesser extent, were apparently bred onto the Norman mares to produce a riding type of great stamina, while 18th- and 19th-century additions of English blood in the form of the Thoroughbred, the Norfolk Trotter, and hunter types led to the formation of the Anglo-Norman; which, judging by appearances, is at least half Thoroughbred.

The original intention behind all this interbreeding seems to have been the production of a quality coach horse, and when motorization threatened the coach horse breeders the focus pivoted to the cavalry remount market. At about this time the split seems to have occurred between the Anglo-Norman saddle horse and the French Trotter.

Selectively bred for the saddle, and improved by top-quality Thoroughbred stallions, the Anglo-Norman has in recent times proved itself an excellent cross-country horse. It is still popular as a cavalry horse, selling annually to the Swiss army; but its most spectacular modern successes are in the worlds of three-day-eventing and showjumping.

Recent improvements, dating from 1965, are giving the Anglo-Norman a new name: the French Saddle Horse. The stud book of the new French Saddle breed is a continuation of the former Anglo-Norman stud book.

FRENCH TROTTER

Origin: France.
Height: About 16.2hh.
Color: Black, bay, brown, chestnut, gray, roan.
Character: Tough, willing, competitive.
Physique: Tall, lightweight horse of good conformation. Neat, alert head; strong shoulder, inclined to be straight; deep chest, prominent withers. Well-coupled body with strong, straight back, and muscular, sloping hindquarters. Legs long and very hard, with rather short cannon bones and hocks well let down.

French Trotter

The French Trotter, also known as the Demi-Sang Trotter, is an offshoot of the Anglo-Norman breed (see French Saddle Horse, above). Trotting races were first held in France in 1836, at Cherbourg, apparently initially for the purpose of choosing the best animals for stud. However, trotting soon became a popular sport, and by the middle of the 19th century it was widespread throughout much of Europe and the United States. Horses were raced in tandem as well as singly. .

Selective breeding through the early part of the 20th century, in which the stallions Young Rattler, Normand, Lavater and Fuchsia were particularly prominent, led to the opening of a Stud Book in 1922. Anglo-Norman horses who could trot 1 kilometer in 1 minute 42 seconds or less, and had proved this ability in a public race, were eligible for the new book. In 1941 the Stud Book was closed to all horses not born of previously-registered parents, and since then the breed of the French Trotter has remained pure.

It is a bigger breed than is usual in a trotting horse. This is because some of the French trotting races are run under the saddle instead of in the shafts, and the French horse must be capable of carrying weights of up to 160lb over quite long distances.

From 5,000–6,000 trotting races are nowadays held annually in France. The biggest race is the Prix d'Amérique at Vincennes, which is a contest of international class.

WURTTEMBERG

Origin: West Germany – Württemberg.
Height: About 16hh.
Color: Usually black, bay, brown, chestnut.
Character: Willing, hard-working, gentle.
Physique: Medium-weight tall cob type, suitable for both harness and saddle work. Straight face, alert expression; good shoulders, roomy chest, deep girth. Straight back with strong loins and good quarters. Clean legs with abundant bone and hard, round feet. A sound, hardy horse with great stamina.

The Württemberg existed as an idea long before it existed as a horse. The breed was developed because of a need for a strong and thrifty animal capable of doing all-round work on small mountain farms. The Württemberg is principally bred at Marbach, a stud founded in 1573, where initial attempts to produce the ideal small-farm worker consisted of crossing Arab stallions onto sturdy local mares. Experiments with East Prussian, Anglo-Norman and Suffolk Punch, as well as with other breeds, did not succeed in stabilizing the type of horse required, and it was not until 1895 that a Stud Book could be opened.

OLDENBURG

Origin: Germany – Oldenburg and East Friesland.
Height: 16.2–17.2hh.
Color: Any solid color – black, brown, bay are the most common.
Character: Precocious horse (matures early); bold, sensible, and kind.
Physique: Tallest and heaviest of the German warm-bloods. Somewhat plain head with straight face. Long, strong neck; powerful, muscular shoulder, chest deep and roomy, deep girth; strong body and hindquarters; legs short with abundant bone, hocks well let down.

Almost all of the great foundation breeds of the taller saddle horses are represented in the pedigree of the Oldenburg. The basis of the breed, which has flourished since the early 17th century, seems to have been strong draught horses of the old Friesian type. To these were added, in the probable following order, Andalusians, Neapolitans, Barbs, English Thoroughbreds, Hanoverians, Cleveland Bays, and Norman/Anglo-Norman horses. This mixture had been incorporated by the turn of the century, at which time the Oldenburg was a prime coach horse type.

After World War I the Oldenburg suffered the usual fate of the coach horse overtaken by the automobile, and the emphasis of the breed was switched to a heavy warm-blood utility animal suitable for cavalry, pack, and light farm work. Mechanization of agriculture brought about a further redundancy and change of type, and the patient breeders of the Oldenburg once more began to change their stock to suit the market. This time

Oldenburg

Thoroughbred and Anglo-Norman stallions were the main influences, with some help from Hanoverian and East Prussian horses.

The result is a strong, all-purpose saddle horse of good conformation; a pleasant mount for the tall rider and a useful horse for eventing and show-jumping.

HANOVERIAN

Origin: West Germany – Hanover and Lower Saxony.
Height: 15.3–17hh.
Color: All solid colors.
Character: Indomitable, courageous animal, intelligent, well-mannered and versatile.
Physique: Somewhat plain head with straight face and intelligent eye, well set on a strong neck. Excellent shoulders; powerful, deep-chested body with broad, strong loins and rounded, muscular quarters. Tail set on high and carried well. Legs short and strong, short in the pasterns, and hocks well let down and flexible. Action straight and showy. A strong, compact horse of good conformation and excellent balance.

Balance, brain and power combine to make the Hanoverian a top-class dressage horse and showjumper, and in these two fields today it justly commands very high prices. Besides its natural aptitude for sporting events – it is also an excellent hunter – it seems to have a genuine love of the game and sometimes an appealing sense of showmanship. The Men's World Showjumping Championship, a quadrennial event, was won in 1974 by Hartwig Steenken of West Germany riding his great liver chestnut Hanoverian mare, Simona, whose capacity to capture an audience was obviously apparent to her. The enormous fences were approached with nonchalance, cleared with a flippant flick of the tail in mid air, left behind with a show of her yellow teeth that seemed an almost human grin of delight. Simona was 16 at the time, an age at which most sporting horses have long been retired from competition.

Hanoverians have been bred since the 17th century, and are one of the oldest of the German warm-blooded breeds. They descend from the famous Hanoverian Creams, also called Isabellas after the Queen of Spain, which were bred under British royal patronage at the Landgestüt at Celle in Hanover and were used as carriage horses for ceremonial purposes. The British royal family of the time was Hanoverian by birth – George I of England was formerly George, Elector of Hanover. Hanoverian Creams were used for British royal processions from the reign of George I to George V, when they were replaced by the Windsor Greys.

The present-day Hanoverian has been modified by Thoroughbred and Trakehner blood.

MECKLENBURG

Origin: East Germany.
Height: 15.2–16.3hh.
Color: All solid colors.
Character: Good saddle horse, willing and bold, with a kind and tractable nature.
Physique: Medium head, well-carried on a strong neck. Powerful shoulders and chest. Deep girth, rounded barrel; compact body with broad, strong loins and good quarters. Legs strong with good bone. Short cannon bones, hard, round hooves. General appearance is that of a slightly smaller Hanoverian.

The Mecklenburg is closely related to the Hanoverian, much the same bloodlines having been used to establish both of them with a frequent exchange of stock between breeders of the two strains. In this century it has been bred as a cavalry remount, though since World War II breeders have tended to concentrate on the production of a good, all-purpose saddle horse.

TRAKEHNER (EAST PRUSSIAN)

Origin: Germany – East Prussia (now Poland).
Height: 16–16.2hh.
Color: Any solid color.

Hanoverian

Mecklenburg

Character: Charming, good-natured, active, intelligent and loyal.

Physique: Attractive saddle horse of good conformation. Somewhat ram-shaped head, broad between the eyes and tapering to a pointed muzzle. Alert, intelligent eye, rather long, pricked ears. Long, strong neck on a good shoulder; prominent withers, deep girth and roomy chest. Medium-length back, strong and well-ribbed-up; good hindquarters. Legs slender and hard, with short cannon bones. Excellent feet. Action extremely good, free-striding and straight. At its best, the Trakehner is a quality show hack.

Trakehnen Stud, now administered by the Polish Ministry of Agriculture, was founded by King Friedrich Wilhelm I of Germany in 1732, when the land on which it stood was part of the province of East Prussia. Horses have been bred there ever since, enriched by imported Arab and Thoroughbred blood. Trakehners have been privately bred in West Germany since the end of World War II, when some 5% of the 25,000 horses registered in the East Prussian Stud Book filtered through as refugees, many of them on foot.

The Trakehner is perhaps the best of the modern West German breeds. It combines good looks and stamina with enormous versatility, and has proved successful in all kinds of sport as well as in dressage, between the shafts, and on the farm.

MASUREN

Origin: Poland (formerly East Prussia).
Height: About 16hh.
Color: All solid colors. Chestnuts and bays are the most common.
Character and Physique: see Trakehner, above.

The Masuren is a continuation of the Trakehner horse left behind by the Germans following their evacuation of Poland in 1945. It has been bred with great skill and care by its new Polish masters, and faithful attention has been and is paid to following the principles used under the old German administration. The result is a splendid saddle horse of great quality, indistinguishable from the Trakehner since it is of identical ancestry.

To all intents and purposes the Masuren and the Trakehner are the same breed – East Prussian. They are divided by only 30 years of separate breeding, and no new blood has been introduced.

HOLSTEIN

Origin: West Germany.
Height: 15.3–16.2hh.
Color: Any solid color. Black, bay and brown are the commonest.
Character: Intelligent, adaptable animal, possessed of spirit and sweet nature. Obedient and willing; very versatile.
Physique: Well-made, somewhat heavily built, horse. Intelligent head on strong neck. Powerful shoulders and chest, prominent withers, deep girth;

Trakehner (East Prussian)

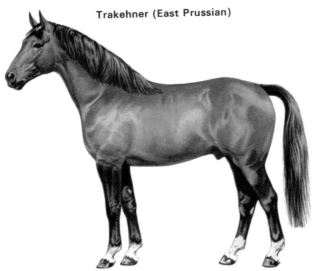

Holstein

compact body, well-ribbed-up; good hindquarters. Rather short legs, with abundant bone. Action straight and long-striding, slightly flamboyant.

This is a splendid all-round animal, combining power, speed and flexibility. Its strong hindquarters and hocks have often helped it to achieve international class in the showjumping arena, while its ability to gallop on, its proud carriage, and its amenity to discipline have led to its success in three-day events. It makes an attractive carriage horse, and its versatility has extended in the past to all-round work on the farm (though nowadays this is hardly economic).

The Holstein is one of the oldest of the warm-bloods, stemming from the 14th-century Marsh Horse, one of the heavy Great Horse types used for medieval warfare. It contains Oriental, Andalusian and Neapolitan blood, with liberal 19th- and 20th-century additions of Thoroughbred and Cleveland Bay.

BEBERBECK

Origin: West Germany.
Height: Usually exceeds 16hh.
Color: Predominantly bay or chestnut.
Character: Even-tempered, willing and enduring; sufficient courage and discipline to make a good cavalry horse, and sufficient patience to work well in harness and on the farm.
Physique: Quality saddle horse, up to weight. Excellent conformation and bone. General appearance similar to the Thoroughbred, though this is a heavier version.

Beberbeck Stud, near Kassel, began in 1720. The original intention was to breed Palomino horses, but this aim seems to have changed to the desire for a quality carriage and riding horse. Initial crosses onto local mares appear to have been made with Arab stallions; later, Thoroughbreds were extensively used. The stud was closed in 1930. The horses are still bred, and are entered in the stud book, but the Beberbeck strain has dwindled numerically and it is no longer an important German breed.

FREIBERGER SADDLE HORSE

Origin: Switzerland.
Height: Usually 15.2–16.1hh.
Color: Any solid color. Gray and blue roan commonest.
Character: Alert, intelligent, willing, docile, and enduring; an excellent saddle horse temperament.
Physique: Medium-sized head showing definite Arab characteristics — large, liquid eye, open nostrils, short, prick ears — carried nobly on crested neck set on good shoulders. Deep girth, well-sprung ribs, short back with good loins and quarters. Clean legs with good bone and short pasterns.

Hard, well-shaped feet. A strong, compact riding horse; active, and showing stamina and endurance.

An elegant new breed of saddle horse, the Freiberger, has been developed at Avenches. It is based on the old Freiberger cold-blood, also called the Franches-Montagnes, which was widely used for agricultural work in Switzerland before mechanization reduced the demand for it, but its elegant appearance indicates that as much as 90% of its parentage is attributable to lightweight warm-bloods. A dominant strain in its ancestry, clearly to be seen in its attractive head, is the Shagya Arabian of Bábolna (see page 138).

EINSIEDLER

Origin: Switzerland.
Height: Roughly 15.3–16.2hh.
Color: Any solid color. Bay and chestnut are the most common.
Character: A bold, active horse, intelligent and tractable and of good disposition. Very versatile.
Physique: Strongly-built lightweight of the Anglo-Norman type (see page 148). Generally good conformation, with powerful shoulders and hindquarters. Action free and straight.

Einsiedler

Because of its versatility, the Einsiedler is in popular demand with the Swiss cavalry, as is its close relation the Anglo-Norman (the Einsiedler is sometimes known as the Swiss Anglo-Norman). It is at once a good jumper, often capable of competition at international level, an adept dressage mount and all-round saddle animal, an outstanding trotter, and a good harness and light agricultural horse.

The horse is named for the Benedictine abbey of Einsiedeln, where records of a stud trace back to 1064. Einsiedlers appear regularly throughout Swiss history, though the breed has fluctuated in type. The modern Einsiedler stems to some extent from imported Hackney horses, but its main influence of change has been the Anglo-Norman.

FURIOSO

Origin: Hungary.
Height: Average 16hh.
Color: Black, dark bay, bay-brown, often with white markings.
Character: Active, intelligent and tractable.
Physique: Handsome saddle/carriage horse. Medium-sized, attractive head, well-carried on long, strong neck. Powerful, sloping shoulder, deep chest, prominent withers. Long, strong back with well-sprung ribs. Muscular, sloping hindquarters, tail rather low set on. Strong, clean legs with hocks well let down and short pasterns. Action free and straight and very slightly exaggerated.

The Furioso is an elegant and versatile saddle horse, popular in its native land and in adjacent countries such as Czechoslovakia, Poland, Austria and Rumania. It excels at dressage and cross-country work, at jumping and eventing, and is used for steeplechasing (Soviet block countries frequently use halfbred horses for this purpose). Additionally, it is an imposing carriage horse, possessing both style and great endurance.

It has been bred in Hungary since the mid-19th century. The foundation sires were an English Thoroughbred named Furioso, foaled in 1836, and a Norfolk Roadster called North Star. These were bred to native mares of the Nonius type.

SWEDISH HALFBRED (SWEDISH WARM-BLOOD)

Origin: Sweden — Flyinge.
Height: Average 16.2hh.
Color: Solid colors; generally chestnut, bay, brown, gray.
Character: Intelligent, bold, good-natured, sensible and obedient.
Physique: Quality saddle horse with excellent conformation. Neat, attractive head with straight face, large eye, and short, pricked ears, well-set on neck of medium length. Shoulder strong and sloping; good withers and depth of girth. Rather deep body, with well-sprung ribs, straight back, good loins, and excellent, rounded hindquarters. Legs hard and slender, with short

Furioso

cannon bones, short, sloping pasterns, and hocks well let down. Action free, straight, and well-balanced.

The Swedish Halfbred, also called Warm-Blood, has its beginnings 300 years ago, when Oriental, Andalusian and Friesian stallions were imported and bred to local mares with the intention of producing good saddle horses for the cavalry. Since then the breed has been carefully built up, using the best of Thoroughbred, East Prussian, Hanoverian, Trakehner and Holstein stallions. The breed is now fixed, and strict controls are exercised over the stallions used. The result is an outstanding saddle horse, a formidable Olympic Games competitor which excels in dressage and jumping.

BAVARIAN WARM BLOOD

Origin: Germany — Lower Bavaria.
Color: Chestnut.
Character and Physique: Heavy warm-blood of medium height, having a deep, broad, powerful body and strong legs with abundant bone. Temperament docile, sensible, willing and enduring.

The esteemed old breed of chestnut war horse, the Rottaler, bred in the fertile valley of Rott in Lower Bavaria and used first as a celebrated battle charger and later as an almost equally celebrated farm and draught animal, has recently given rise to the new Bavarian Warm Blood. Modification of the Rottaler has been going on for a couple of centuries, using Thoroughbred, Cleveland Bay and Norman bloodlines, and more recently those of the Oldenburg.

About 1960 the name Rottaler was discontinued, and the breed has since been known as the Bavarian Warm Blood.

GELDERLAND

Origin: Holland — Gelderland.
Height: Usually 15.2—16hh; occasionally taller.
Color: Solid colors. Chestnut and gray are commonest.
Character: Docile, good-natured and very active.
Physique: Somewhat plain head with convex face and intelligent expression, carried gaily on strong, arched neck. Good shoulders. Compact, strong body, broad and deep. Powerful hindquarters, with tail set on high and held with exaggerated carriage. Legs short and strong, with short cannon bones and hocks well let down. Round, hard feet. Stylish action, typical of a good carriage horse.

This attractive breed stems from a variety of sources, notably Andalusian, Norman and Norfolk Roadster. During the last century Hackney, Oldenburg, East Friesian and Anglo-Norman blood has been introduced and the best of the offspring interbred in an intelligent campaign to fix a new breed.

The Gelderland makes a first-class carriage horse, combining presence, good conformation and an attractive, showy action. It is also capable of light agricultural work. It is a pleasant horse to ride, and its power and thrust have proved it to be an above-average showjumper.

NONIUS

Origin: Hungary.
Height: Large Nonius — over 15.3hh. Small Nonius — under 15.3hh.
Color: Black, dark bay, dark brown.
Character: Excellent temperament: willing, consistent, calm, kind and active.
Physique: Bold, attractive head, with kind eye, open nostril, and alert ears, well-set on long, strong neck. Good, strong shoulder and good withers; barrel rounded with a rather broad back and loins and well-sprung ribs. Good hindquarters and hard legs with short pasterns. Round, small hooves. A compact carriage/saddle horse, active and free-striding; very tough.

This medium-heavy all-purpose horse is a forerunner of the Furioso (see page 160), which it closely resembles. Both originated on the Mezöhegyes Stud in Hungary. The Nonius is now also bred in Yugoslavia, Rumania and Czechoslovakia.

Gelderland

Nonius

The Nonius is believed to descend from a prepotent and prolific French stallion called Nonius, who was foaled about 1810 in Normandy from a Norman mare by an English halfbred. Nonius's progeny while standing at Mezöhegyes is said to have exceeded 200 animals suitable for stud.

The modern Nonius has many uses, ranging from sport through carriage to agriculture. Outcrossed to lighter breeds such as the Thoroughbred, it produces first-class hunters, eventers and showjumpers.

EAST FRIESIAN

Origin: East Germany — Thuringia.
Height: About 16–16.2hh.
Color: Any solid color.
Character: Bold, spirited, kind — an excellent riding temperament.
Physique: Quality saddle/carriage horse, similar to the Oldenburg but having a more refined, "breedy" head and a somewhat lighter frame.

Until the division of Germany at the end of World War II the East Friesian and the Oldenburg were one and the same, and horses from the provinces of Oldenburg and East Friesland were regularly exchanged and interbred. During the last 30 years this free exchange has not been so easy, and the East Friesian has developed along rather different lines from its sibling. Arabian blood from the stud at Marbach, West Germany, and Hungarian Arab from Bábolna have helped to refine the East Friesian's body, reduce its height, and improve its formerly somewhat plain head; more recently, Hanoverian stallions have added compactness and strength to the breed.

DANUBIAN

Origin: Bulgaria.
Height: About 15.2hh.
Color: Black, dark chestnut.
Character: Active, docile, indomitable, energetic.
Physique: Strong, compact, handsome animal with a neat, expressive head, well-set on strong neck. Massive shoulder, deep, strong body, and powerful hindquarters with tail set on rather high. Legs comparatively slender for bulk of the body, but hard and of dense bone. General effect is of power and vigor without coarseness.

The Danubian is a 20th-century product of the State stud near Pleven. It was developed from Nonius stallions crossed with Anglo-Arab mares; and, surprisingly, it seems to be thought of mainly as a draught horse, though maybe this is not so odd because its dense, muscular body can pull comparatively enormous weights and its aristocratic bloodlines give it the will-power to triumph. It is also a good saddle horse and a useful jumper, especially when crossed with the Thoroughbred.

East Friesian

Danubian

EAST BULGARIAN

Origin: Bulgaria.
Height: Average 15.3hh.
Color: Chestnut, black.
Character: Ideal saddle horse – active, intelligent and good-natured.
Physique: Neat, attractive head with straight face. Good, sloping shoulder, roomy chest, deep girth. Longish body with well-sprung ribs, straight back, good loins. Muscular hindquarters. Legs clean and of good bone. An elegant saddle horse, from its appearance an obvious Anglo-Arab of predominantly Thoroughbred type. It is hardy, active, and a good mover.

Bred at the Vassil Kolarov state farm near Shumen and at Stefan Karadja, the State stud in Dobrudja, the East Bulgarian is the product of selected Thoroughbred, halfbred, Arab and Anglo-Arab bloodlines. The breed was fixed in the first part of the 20th century, and since then only Thoroughbred blood has been added.

As with many of the European hot-bloods, it is expected to work in agriculture as well as under saddle. Selective breeding for performance of all kinds has made it extremely versatile, though its greatest aptitude is for sport. It excels at dressage and eventing, and has also the guts and stamina to take part in international steeplechasing. As a 'chaser it lacks the turn of foot of the Thoroughbred and cannot fairly compete with it; but on tricky endurance courses such as that of the famous Grand Pardubice in Czechoslovakia, where two-thirds of the 4½ miles is run on plough and the 31 fences include every conceivable kind of obstacle, the handiness and level-headedness of the East Bulgarian puts it well on terms with its faster, flightier rival.

GERMAN TROTTER

Origin: West Germany.
Height: About 15.3hh.
Color: Solid colors.
Character: Bold, active, competitive, enduring.
Physique: Rather handsome small horse with expressive head. Strong, well developed, slightly upright shoulder; prominent withers, deep girth, robust body with well-sprung ribs; lean, muscular quarters. Legs fine and iron hard. Hard feet. Splendid, long-striding action.

Trotting is more popular in Germany than Thoroughbred racing, and there are roughly twice as many trotters as racehorses. The beginnings of the craze occurred in the second half of the 19th century, and the first trotting club, the Altona, was formed in Hamburg in 1874.

Russian Orlov Trotters were the basis of the modern German breed, which has since been massively improved by American Standardbred blood and more recently by that of the French Trotter. Performance is kept to a high

East Bulgarian

German Trotter

standard through a system of handicapping based on the amount of prize money won, which in turn is based on individual speed over 1,000 metres. Trotters eligible for the standard register are those with times of under 1 minute 30 seconds, and there is an élite register for those who have achieved 1 minute 20 seconds or less. The record over 1,000 metres is 1 minute 17.3 seconds. The record-holder is Permit, who is by Epilog, most famous of the German Trotter sires.

FREDERIKSBORG

Origin: Denmark.
Height: 15.2–16.1hh.
Color: Usually chestnut.
Character: Active, tractable, willing; a hard worker.
Physique: Strong harness horse type. Head somewhat plain, often with a convex face; but eye intelligent and general expression alert. Head carried well on strong neck; huge, extremely powerful shoulder and big chest. Deep girth with rounded barrel and broad back; loins and quarters strong and muscled. Good legs with plenty of bone, and hocks well let down.

The Frederiksborg bears an old and noble name. It has its roots in the Royal Fredericksborg Stud, which was founded in 1562 by King Frederick II and was at the time the leading establishment for the provision of school horses to European royal stables. Horses – the stock was largely Andalusian and Neapolitan – were trained in the high school Airs and performed brilliantly both under saddle and as carriage horses. Demand for the newly-created Frederiksborg to improve other breeds was high for several centuries – so much so that the stud was dissolved in 1839 because there were not enough horses left to breed from.

The modern Frederiksborg's connection with the old breed is tenuous. Fortunately there were enough Frederiksborgs left in Denmark after the short-sighted closure of 1839 for the breed to be continued, but much outside blood was needed to build up the numbers. In 1923 the breed began to be registered again, and since then it has flourished and is now widespread throughout Denmark. It is an excellent light draught/harness horse and is also in use under saddle.

KNABSTRUP

Origin: Denmark.
Height: About 15.3hh.
Color: Exclusively a spotted horse, marked in the usual Appaloosa patterns on a roan base.

The Knabstrup dates from the Napoleonic Wars, when a spotted mare named Flaebehoppen was acquired from a Spanish army officer. Put to a Frederiksborg stallion, she became the foundation mare of a breed that was to become extremely popular.

Frederiksborg

Knabstrup

Unfortunately, Knabstrups have been carelessly crossed in recent times, with efforts being extended towards good spotted patterns only and little regard paid to conformity of type. It is therefore doubtful whether it can any longer be called a breed. At its best it was — and one hopes still is — a horse very similar to the Frederiksborg, though lighter in build.

CHAROLLAIS HALFBRED

Origin: France.
Height: 15–16.2hh.
Color: Solid colors.

This is an attractive, strongly-built lightweight with a kind, intelligent disposition. Nowadays it is used as a hunter, for which function it is greatly praised; but it was popular previously as a cavalry remount and artillery horse.

The Charollais Halfbred owes its quality to Thoroughbred and Anglo-Norman blood. It is bred along almost identical lines with the Nivernais and Bourbonnais Halfbreds, and these three types are so similar that they are usually known collectively as the *Demi-Sang Charollais*.
See also Limousin Halfbred.

LIMOUSIN HALFBRED

Origin: France.
Height: Average 16hh.
Color: Solid colors — chestnut and bay are the most usual.

The Limousin Halfbred is one of the many good halfbred horses which have become a specialty of France. Collectively, they are known under the rather loose title of *Cheval de Selle Français* (not to be confused with the Anglo-Norman), though they are subdivided into groups according to their location — the Limousin and Charollais, for instance, are part of the group known as the *Demi-Sang du Centre*. The modern aim behind these halfbreds is the production of good, all-purpose saddle horses.

The Limousin Halfbred is a quality horse of Anglo-Arab type, with a definite oriental cast. It originates from a foundation stock of the best Limousin mares mingled for some hundred years with Thoroughbred, Arab and Anglo-Arab stallions. Some modern Limousins possess Anglo-Norman blood.

FRIESIAN

Origin: Holland — Province of Friesland.
Height: About 15hh.
Color: Black — no other color is permitted, and even white markings are considered undesirable.
Character: Exceptionally pleasant temperament — sweet-natured, willing

and hardworking. Has excited comments such as "cheerful", "loyal" and "very sensitive."

Physique: Fine, rather long, alert head with small ears, carried high on a crested neck. Body very strong and compact, with prominent shoulder, rounded barrel and hindquarters. Rather short, sturdy legs with colossal bone and feather on heels. Hard, open hooves. Exceptional growth of mane and tail — mane said sometimes to reach the ground. The action active and somewhat flamboyant, and the horse bears itself with pride.

Keeping in mind that the horses of yesterday bear scant resemblance to today's favored breeds, the Friesian is one of the oldest and most consistently popular horses in Europe. There is evidence in Friesland of a prehistoric cold-blood which was used as a domestic animal as long as 3,000 years ago. Later descendants (presumably) of this heavy native animal were valued as saddle horses by the medieval nobility, and are portrayed by many of the Dutch Old Masters. It is probable that by this time the Friesian had been strongly enriched with Andalusian blood, and Oriental influences are also likely.

The 19th-century craze for trotting seems to have influenced breeders of the Friesian towards a lighter, faster type of horse which, while full of promise for the racetrack, would have declined in ability as an agricultural worker, and it is possibly because of this that the breed came very close to

Friesian

extinction just before World War I. At that time, numbers·were so much reduced that only three Friesian stallions were left, and it is only because a few Dutch farmers spotted the emergency in the nick of time and took prompt and clever action that the Friesian survives today. Oldenburg stallions were imported to help build up the depleted stock.

A strong revival of the Friesian occurred during World War II, when motorized vehicles fell into short supply and fuel was strictly rationed. The demand for horses in agriculture rose sharply; Friesians were particularly suited to adapt to any kind of work required of them, and so their numbers were quickly increased. In 1954 Queen Juliana of the Netherlands honored the Friesian breed society with the title "Royal."

Nowadays the Friesian is popular in harness (often in the show ring, where it sometimes causes a kind of patriotic nostalgia), in the circus (because of its striking carriage and willingness to adapt itself), and under the saddle; but its first function remains supreme — it is a "cheerful, loyal, and very sensitive" all-round working horse.

GRONINGEN

Origin: Holland — Groningen.
Height: 15.2–16hh. Can be taller.
Color: Usually black, bay, dark brown, often with white markings.
Character: Gentle, obedient, willing, enduring.
Physique: Handsome head with straight face, intelligent eye, and rather long ears. Powerful, deep body with broad chest and strong shoulders and hindquarters. Tail set on high and carried well. Legs strong and clean, with short cannon bones. An attractive light draught/heavy saddle breed; a frugal horse to keep, having a sound constitution and ability to work well on a meager diet. Action stylish, suitable to a good carriage horse.

The kind nature of the Groningen makes it an excellent animal for all-round farm work and for riding. The breed is developed from the heavier Friesian crossed with East Friesian and Oldenburg horses. Unfortunately it has now become rare.

MAREMMANA

Origin: Italy.
Height: About 15.3hh.
Color: Solid colors.
Character: Calm, active, intelligent, patient.
Physique: Strong, hard, rather heavy saddle/light draught horse, frugal and enduring.

The Maremmana, sometimes called Maremma, is a horse ridden by the Italian mounted police. It is also of service to agriculture, and is much favored by the *butteri* (cowboys) who herd the cattle. It is an indigenous Italian breed.

Groningen

SARDINIAN

Origin: Sardinia.
Height: 15–15.2hh. Can be smaller, but is rarely taller.
Color: Bay and brown are the usual colors.
Character and Physique: Small, tough horse of good conformation. Bold, clever, and enduring, extremely hardy and sure-footed. Action is clean and straight.

The Sardinian, as its name implies, is an island breed. It is used largely by the mounted police and as a general saddle horse. With training, it can be taught to jump to show standard, and it has in the past participated in international competition as a member of the Italian Army team.

MURGESE

Origin: Italy.
Height: 15–16hh.
Color: Usually chestnut.

This horse bears a famous name, since the Murge district was renowned for centuries for its excellent saddle horses. About 200 years ago the Murgese breed died out, apparently from lack of local interest. The modern Murgese is not related to this illustrious forerunner.

The Murgese of today is a light draught/saddle horse. It is not yet strictly uniform in type. At its best it is a distinctive riding horse, showing obvious traces of Oriental blood.

CALABRESE

Origin: Italy — Calabria.
Height: About 16hh.
Color: Any solid color.

The Calabrese is a handsome, medium-weight saddle horse which is bred in the south of Italy. It has a rather small, alert head and a compact body with strong shoulders and hindquarters. It is now decreasing in numbers.

SALERNO

Origin: Italy — Maremma and Salerno.
Height: About 16hh.
Color: Any solid color.
Character: Intelligent, responsive, gentle.
Physique: Slightly large head showing definite quality. Good shoulders and quarters, prominent withers, and ample room in the chest. Bone is good, and general conformation is attractive.

The Salerno, a favorite of the Italian army, is now on the decline. It is a high-quality saddle horse, showing aristocratic ancestry.

PLATEAU PERSIAN

Iran has been producing exquisite small riding horses for more than 2,500 years. The animals are akin to the desert Arabian, and show much the same elegance and fire and air — hardly surprising, since they were produced by the same ruthless natural selection, nurtured in the same inhospitable climate, fed a diet that was often meager, and conditioned in a tough and harsh terrain.

On the central Persian plateau, a rough mountain country inhabited by nomadic tribes, several similar strains of horse have come into being over the centuries. Among them are the Shirazi, Quashquai, Basseri, Bakhtiari and some Persian Arab types. Very recently these horses have been grouped together by the Royal Horse Society of Iran under the single heading Plateau Persian. Two of the most popular of the Plateau Persian strains are the Darashouri and the Jaf; but before these are described mention must be made of a horse that is not a Plateau Persian at all but a new breed created from it — the Pahlavan.

The Pahlavan, bred primarily by HIM the Shah, is a Thoroughbred-

Salerno

Plateau Persian-Arab cross standing 15.2–16hh and possessing strength, elegance and great beauty. Also in the Imperial stables is another tall, strong horse that is gaining popularity in Iran – the Anglo-Persian, whose blood-lines need no explaining.

TCHENARAN

Origin: Iran.
Height: About 15hh.
Color: Any solid color.
Character: Spirited, willing, active, enduring, docile.
Physique: Alert, elegant.head with large, liquid eye, carried gaily on an arched neck. Good, sloping shoulder, prominent withers; compact body, with good loins and strong hindquarters. Hard legs and feet. Action straight and airy. A tough little horse, possessing both courage and stamina.

The Tchenaran is the product of a Plateau Persian stallion and a Turkoman mare, as a mule is a cross between a horse and a donkey, or an Anglo-Arab a cross between a Thoroughbred and an Arab. As such, it is not usual to breed a Tchenaran to a Tchenaran, since the offspring tends to deteriorate in quality. Curiously, crossing a Turkoman stallion onto a Plateau Persian mare does not produce a foal of such high caliber, and for this reason the opposite cross is always used.

Tchenaran

Tchenarans have been bred since at least the 18th century. They make excellent saddle horses, beautiful, adaptable and bold, and were until recently much in demand by the cavalry.

DARASHOURI

Origin: Iran — Province of Fars.
Height: Average 15hh.
Color: Chestnut, bay, brown, gray; occasionally black.
Character: Intelligent, spirited, friendly and docile.
Physique: Splendid, silky-coated, lightweight saddle horse of excellent conformation, similar to the Arab in appearance and action. At once elegant and tough.

JAF

Origin: Iran — Kurdistan.
Height: Usually over 15hh, but it can vary.
Color: Chestnut, bay, brown, gray; occasionally black.
Character: Courageous, intelligent; both gentle and fiery.
Physique: Very attractive Oriental saddle horse of Arab type. A tough, wiry horse, typical of the sort bred in a harsh mountain/desert terrain. Hard feet. Like the Darashouri, it has great powers of endurance.

Darashouri

Jaf

IOMUD

Origin: USSR — Central Asia.
Height: About 14.2–15hh.
Color: Any solid color. Gray is commonest, then chestnut and bay.
Character: Great courage and endurance; adaptable.
Physique: Slim head with straight or concave face, large eyes, prick ears, well set on a longish neck. Good shoulder, prominent withers, and a strong, straight back. Sinewy hindquarters with a look of elastic power. Legs long, hard, and slender. Coat fine, and mane and tail thin and silky. Similar to its relative the Akhal-Teké, though less greyhound-like, fractionally smaller, and more close-coupled.

The Iomud is a strain of Turkoman, like the Akhal-Teké, though it is possessed of more stamina, is not as fleet-footed, and is more similar to the Arab in appearance. It is extremely adaptable, and makes a good cross-country horse on any terrain. It is untiring in distance races, and has the courage and quality needed for a good cavalry animal.

AKHAL-TEKE

Origin: USSR — Turkoman Steppes.
Height: 14.2–15.2hh.
Color: The prevailing color is gold, either as golden dun, golden bay, or golden chestnut, and the coat often has a metallic bloom. Other colors occur — gray and bay are quite common. Sometimes has white markings.
Character: Bold, self-willed. Can be obstinate and bad-tempered.
Physique: Delicate head with long, straight face, large, expressive eye, long ears. Long, thin neck, set high on an excellent, sloping shoulder. Very pronounced withers. Tendency to narrow chest. Body long, lean, narrow and sinewy, with pronounced croup and sloping hindquarters. Tail low-set. Legs long and hard and sinewy. Mane and tail short and sparse and very silky, and in some instances there is virtually no mane or forelock. General effect is of the sinewy grace of a greyhound. Magnificent action, free and flowing; in all paces a soft, gliding, elastic stride.

The Akhal-Teké is the most distinctive strain of the ancient race of horses known as Turkoman, or Turkmene, which have played such a successful part in the mounted warfare of the past 2,000–3,000 years. Akhal-Tekés have been bred separately since time out of mind — there are indications of a horse of the Akhal-Teké type existing as long ago as 500 BC.

They are supremely resilient horses, conditioned by centuries of exposure to extremes of heat and cold in the deserts of central Asia. An Akhal-Teké is reported to have crossed 900 miles of desert without a drink of water; and a famous 1935 trek from Ashkabad to Moscow (2,672 miles) involving Akhal-Teké and Iomud horses included 225 miles of desert which were covered in a waterless three days.

Akhal-Teke

Iomud

As with all breeds of horses which are the prized possession of nomadic desert tribes, Akhal-Tekés have been subjected to some curious methods of handling. They were often kept swathed in blankets throughout the year, and were fed a concentrated diet including such unlikely things as mutton fat. These practices continue into the present day: the Akhal-Teké is valued as a racehorse and is kept in training wearing the traditional seven blankets (each of which has a separate name) and eating a light, high-protein diet. Clothing is worn at all times except during the brief intervals of racing, breeding, and for a few minutes at sundown to air the horse's skin. Horses in training are fed eggs and butter mixed with barley, also bread dough fried in butter.

The Akhal-Teké is potentially the best of the many magnificent Russian saddle horses. It has speed, grace and versatility, and is marred only by its self-assertive temperament. It is a superb jumper on its day, though when the mood takes it wrong it will refuse and there is little its rider can do to change its mind; it has a natural bent for dressage – the gold medal for the Grand Prix de Dressage at the Rome Olympics (1960) was won by an Akhal-Teké stallion.

The Turkoman, and in particular its offshoot the Akhal-Teké, is very possibly the ancestor of the Arab.

DON

Origin: USSR – Central Asia.
Height: 15.1–15.3hh.
Color: Any solid color – usually chestnut, bay, gray, or golden.
Character: Energetic, calm, consistent.
Physique: Medium-sized head of the Thoroughbred type, wideset intelligent eyes, straight face, smallish ears; neck somewhat long and straight, good withers and rather upright shoulder, roomy chest. Back straight and rather broad, with well-sprung ribs; hindquarters strong. Legs long and hard, though tending to be straight behind, pasterns often upright. Astonishing stamina and endurance. Action inclined to be a little short and inelegant.

This former Cossack horse was extensively used in the raids on Napoleon's defeated army during its long retreat from Moscow throughout the bitter winter of 1812. Food was scarce, and what there was of it was of poor quality, but though most of the French horses died of weakness the little Cossack horses galloped in again and again to the attack and when the French were finally gone were ridden the long way home to Moscow. It was an inelegant little animal, light-framed and tough and wiry; but for courage and endurance it was equal to the Arab.

The Don was the favourite horse of the Cossacks, and as such was an important cavalry mount. It was not a pampered animal. It was (and still is) herded on the central Asian steppes, where it must forage for survival in the heavy winter snows.

Today the Don is taller and of better conformation. During the 19th

Don

century, Turkoman, Karabakh, Karabair and other stallions of the Oriental type were loosed to run with it on the steppes, doing much to improve the Don's appearance. Subsequently Thoroughbred and Orlov stallions were bred to it, which gave it height. The result is a quality saddle horse which has unusual stamina.

BUDYONNY

Origin: USSR.
Height: 15.2–16hh.
Color: Chestnut and bay, usually with the golden sheen shown by so many Russian saddle horses. Brown and black also occur.
Character: Intelligent, calm, energetic.
Physique: Superb saddle horse, robust and elegant. Head neat and dry with large, expressive eyes and small ears, carried well on a long and often crested neck set high on a strong shoulder with prominent withers. Body close-coupled, deep-girthed, with strong loins and quarters. Legs rather long and slender, hard and of excellent proportion and bone. Hooves round and hard. Moves well.

The Budyonny is named for a famous Russian cavalry leader of the Revolution, Marshal Budyonny, who instigated this breed almost half a century ago at the Army stud at Rostov. The original cross, and the main bloodlines of today, was Thoroughbred-Don, which was at first known as Anglo-Don. For no known reason, Thoroughbred stallions on Don mares produce better offspring than Don stallions on Thoroughbred mares. Other blood such as Kazakh and Kirgiz was also used. The best of the progeny was very carefully reared and submitted to tests for speed and endurance, aptitude, comfort, fertility, and so on; and thus the new breed got away to a highly-selective start. By 1948 it was fixed and recognized.

The Budyonny was originally planned as the perfect cavalry horse, though there is not much call for it in that field today. It is used for many purposes, but excels at dressage, steeplechasing, and all equestrian sports.

KARABAKH

Origin: USSR — Karabakh Mountains, Azerbaidzhan.
Height: 14–14.3hh.
Color: Dun, chestnut, bay, usually with a golden sheen. Also gray.
Character: Energetic, tough, active, calm.
Physique: Small, fine head with broad forehead and large eyes, small muzzle, prick ears; strong, well-made neck, good shoulder, prominent withers; strong, compact body, well-ribbed-up, good quarters with tail fairly low-set; legs fine for its bulk, hard and clean and well made. Excellent feet. Action is easy and gentle, comfortable for the rider.

This mountain breed is of great antiquity. It was known and valued as long as 1,500 years ago, and is believed to contain Türkoman, Arab and Persian blood. In its turn it has had influence on other Russian breeds, the Don especially, and during the 18th century it reached a peak of popularity and was widely exported. A few have been imported into England, notably by HM Queen Elizabeth II. Unfortunately, it is now becoming rare.

The slightly taller Karadagh of north-west Iran, bred just across the border from Azerbaidzhan, is thought to be the same horse. Not many of these remain, either.

KABARDIN

Origin: USSR — Caucasus.
Height: 14.2–15.1hh.
Color: Usually bay, but can be black, dark brown, gray.
Character: Calm, intelligent, independent; possesses strong homing instinct.
Physique: Intelligent head with straight face; tips of ears turn slightly inwards. Strong body with good front and prominent withers. Back straight and somewhat long, hindquarters good. Very hard legs and feet. Has a tendency to sickle hocks, which occur more often than not. Coat fine, mane and tail usually wavy. Free-moving, sturdy horse with endurance; exceptionally sure-footed, very long-lived.

Budyonny

Karabakh

The Kabardin comes from the mountains of the northern Caucasus area, and like all mountain breeds is distinctive for its sure-footedness and for its readiness to tackle paths that most horses would think unpassable. It is used as a pack and saddle animal, and the mares are valued for their milk.

The Kabardin's background is uncertain. It seems to have arisen from a tough native stock, possibly Mongolian, and to have been improved with southern blood of the Turkoman and Arab strains.

LOKAI

Origin: USSR − Uzbekistan.
Height: 14–14.3hh.
Color: Usually bay, gray, chestnut; black and dun rare. Sometimes a golden sheen to coat.
Character: Tractable, willing, brave.
Physique: Varies. Head can be light or heavyish, and the face straight or convex; intelligent eye, short ears, straight neck. Good shoulder. Body well-ribbed-up, with straight back and quarters often sloping. Hard legs with good bone, but some tendency to splay in front and to sickle hocks behind. Hard feet. Mane and tail sparse, and sometimes wavy or curly.

This is a tough mountain horse, widely used for pack and transport in the high areas of Tadzhikstan. It was originally bred in the 16th century by the Lokai tribe of Uzbekistan, and has since been made taller and handsomer by injections of Iomud, Karabair, and other Russian and Eastern blood.

Its courage and stamina suit it to sporting events. It is used for racing (it is not very fast), endurance tests, and for pastimes such as hawking and hunting. Its most spectacular sporting achievements are in the national game of *kop-kopi* (goat-snatching), in which a mounted man carrying a goat is pursued by others who try to take it away from him.

NEW KIRGIZ

Origin: USSR − Kirgiz and Kazakhstan.
Height: 14.1–15.1hh.
Color: Mostly bay, gray, chestnut.
Character: Docile, active, tough, adaptable.
Physique: Small, dry head with prick ears; long neck well-set on strong but upright shoulder. Body muscular but rather long, with straight back, good withers and loins, and sloping·croup. Legs short and hard, with abundant bone. A hardy, free-moving horse, sure-footed and with great stamina.

This new development, based on the ancient Kirgiz horse, has been specially bred as an all-purpose saddle and harness horse. Complex outcrossing for specific qualities, followed by selective crossing of the offspring thus obtained, began about 1930 and has led to the breed called New Kirgiz.

Kabardin

Lokai

185

New Kirgiz

The end product is in fact only about 25% Kirgiz, the remaining three-quarters being Don and Thoroughbred in the ratio of roughly two parts to one.

 .The New Kirgiz is a splendid mountain horse, able to fulfill all kinds of functions in harness, under the saddle and in sport, and in addition it is fertile, frugal, and a provider of good milk for *kumiss*.

KUSTANAIR

Origin: USSR – Kazakhstan.
Height: 15–15.2hh.
Color: Solid colors, usually bay or chestnut.
Character: Intelligent, adaptable.
Physique: There are three types: the Steppe, which is massive; the Saddle, which is light and airy; and the Basic, which is somewhere between the two. Hard, handsome horse, with short legs and plenty of bone. Medium-sized head on long neck; prominent withers, strong but upright shoulder, well-coupled body with sloping, muscular hindquarters. Has good action, great stamina, is hardy and adaptable.

Interest on the part of the cavalry in the latter part of the 19th century stimulated the improvement of the small, hardy horses which ran in herds in the harsh climate of Kazakhstan. Good food and care increased the height quite quickly from about 13hh to over 14hh, and later improvements were made by outcrossing with Thoroughbred, Don and other breeds.

The three types of Kustanair together offer a wide range of performance under saddle and in harness.

KARABAIR

Origin: USSR — Uzbekistan.
Height: 15–15.3hh.
Color: Solid colors — usually gray, bay, chestnut.
Character: Intelligent, responsive, sensible and brave.
Physique: There are three types of Karabair — the Saddle, which is fast, elegant and strong; the Harness, which is massive and long-backed; and the Saddle/Harness type, a compromise between the two. The horse has a rather dry head with alert expression and definite look of Oriental blood. Body strong, especially in the shoulders, back straight, hindquarters broad and sloping. Legs strong and clean, though sometimes sickle-hocked. Mane and tail thin. The horse moves well and freely, is hardy and adaptable. Because of its variation in type it can range from coarse to beautiful.

The Karabair is another ancient mountain breed, of great service to farming in Central Asia. As a riding horse it is keen and competitive, figuring prominently in the many mounted equestrian games beloved by the Russians of this area.

TORIC

Origin: USSR — Estonia.
Height: 15–15.2hh.
Color: Mainly chestnut; also bay.
Character: Good-natured, calm, hardworking and enduring.
Physique: Strong harness horse with good conformation. Attractive head of medium size, with bold eye and mobile ears; strong neck, set high on muscular shoulder; deep girth, strong back, body dense with well-sprung ribs, powerful hindquarters; legs short and hard, with abundant bone, short cannon bones, short pasterns, light feather on heels. Well-shaped feet. Action free, straight and even.

This is a strong harness and general working horse, popular on the farms of northern Russia. The breed was developed during the late 19th and early 20th centuries. The basis for the Toric was the local Klepper, an indigenous native horse of unspecified type. To this was added a wide variety of native and foreign blood which included that of the Arab, Ardennais, East Friesian, Hackney, Hanoverian, Orlov Trotter, Thoroughbred and Trakhener. The result is a handsome, light draught sort with abundant capacity for work.

ORLOV TROTTER

Origin: USSR.
Height: 15.2–17hh; average 15.3hh.
Color: Solid colors. Gray and black are most usual.
Character: Active, bold, courageous.
Physique: Powerful and thick-set, with generally good conformation. Varies somewhat in type. Head usually a little heavy, but with an Oriental cast; large eyes, short ears. Strong, rather upright shoulder, good withers, roomy chest. Girth deep, ribs well-sprung; back long, flat, broad, with strong loins and muscular quarters. Very hard legs with abundant bone. Thick mane and tail, feather on fetlocks (often quite heavy). Strong constitution, fertile and long-lived. Excellent action.

This popular horse, probably the best-known outside Russia of all the Soviet breeds, is the brainchild of Count Alexius Grigorievich Orlov, a man of great military talent and an early revolutionary who may have been the murderer of Czar Peter III. In 1777 Count Orlov crossed his Arab stallion, Smetanka, with a Dutch or Danish mare and got a colt called Polkan. Bred to a black Dutch mare, Polkan sired a horse called Bars I, who is considered to be the true foundation sire of the Orlov Trotter. Other blood, including Arab, Thoroughbred, Mecklenburg and Norfolk Trotter, has since been added. The new breed was for many years known as the Russian Trotter.

Trotting is immensely popular in Russia, and a good horse must travel well and adjust easily to the pronounced climatic variations which are to be expected in this huge nation. There are more than 30,000 Orlovs, bred at 34 State studs, and though they are not as fast as the American Standard-bred (the Orlov record is a mile in 2.02 minutes) they provide excellent competitive entertainment. They are also used under the saddle in many sports, and make good cavalry horses.

LATVIAN HARNESS HORSE

Origin: USSR – Latvia.
Height: 15.2–16hh.
Color: Usually bay, dark brown, or chestnut.
Character: Calm, sensible, good-natured, hard-working.
Physique: Powerful, muscular horse of good conformation. Head large, with a straight face, kind eyes, and short ears. Strong, crested neck, set rather high on massive, sloping shoulders with well-defined withers, deep chest, and girth. Back straight and strong, barrel round and hard, hindquarters muscular and ample. Strong legs with much bone. Abundant mane and tail, and light feather on heels.

There are three types of Latvian: the basic type shown in the illustration, to which 85% of them belong, a taller harness type and a lighter type which has less bone and which looks more like a trotter.

Orlov Trotter

Latvian Harness Horse

The Latvian Harness Horse is an all-purpose breed popular throughout the Soviet Union. In the south it is thought of mainly as a draught horse while in the north its main uses are under the saddle and in harness. It is also widely used to work on farms, and takes part in pulling contests and endurance tests in accordance with the common European and Soviet practice of proving a horse before he is put to stud.

The original Latvian horse has existed on its home ground since before recorded history began. It seems to have been a typical example of the basic Forest cold-blood type of Northern Europe. From the 17th century on it has been crossed extensively with warm-bloods of all kinds – many of the German saddle breeds, Arabs, and even Thoroughbreds contributed to it, and during the early part of the breed's improvement heavy horses were also used. The breed was finally fixed in 1952.

METIS TROTTER

Origin: USSR.
Height: Average 15.3hh.
Color: Solid colors – gray, black, chestnut. bay; other colors rare.
Character and Physique: Brave, tough horse of good conformation, though inclined to an upright shoulder. Type not yet fixed, but characteristic of both its parent bloodlines.

The Métis Trotter is a cross between the best of the Orlovs and American Standardbreds. The breed was begun in the early 1950s, and is not yet fixed.

SOKOLSKY

Origin: Poland and USSR.
Height: 15–16hh.
Color: Any solid color. Chestnut is by far the most common.
Character: Kind, patient, calm, hard-working.
Physique: Large head with straight face, kind eye, and mobile ears. Strong, clean neck. Powerful front: well-developed, sloping shoulder, deep chest and girth, prominent withers. Back fairly short and straight, hindquarters strong and sloping. Hard legs, almost devoid of feather, short cannon bones, strong tendons, large, round feet.

The Sokólsky is a useful working horse for the small farmer. It has a strong constitution and is a frugal horse to keep. It adapts to almost any sort of work, and is a willing worker.

DØLE-GUDBRANDSDAL

Origin: Norway.
Height: 14.2–15.2hh.

Color: Solid colors — almost always black, brown, bay.
Character: Active, patient, adaptable.
Physique: Varies from a muscular draught type to a much lighter-weight animal reminiscent of the Fell pony. Characteristics are a neat, somewhat pony-type head with straight face, set well on a neck with slight to marked crest; strong shoulder, often a little upright, deep girth; strong body, well-ribbed-up, and powerful, round hindquarters; legs short and of abundant bone, with moderate to heavy feather, depending on heaviness of type. Action straight, and especially good at the trot. Hardy and enduring.

The average Døle-Gudbrandsdal horse (average meaning middleweight) is very like the Dales pony of England, and there are also strong reminders of the Friesian. All derive from the same North Sea stock, and very probably were interchanged from country to country before the history of horse breeds was considered worthy of record.

The Døle is easily the most influential and most widespread breed in Norway. Varying as it does in type — and this is probably owing to out-crossing with differing types of foreign stock, ranging from heavy draught to the Thoroughbred — it can perform all of the tasks required by farmer, carter, lumberman and also be an economic, sure-footed saddle horse.

The demand for Døle horses, steady throughout the first part of the 20th century, reached an artificial high in World War II because of scarcity of

Døle-Gudbrandsdal

motor fuel. Demand for heavy horses has since declined, and today there is a call for lighter animals of the riding type. Government-controlled studs were started in 1962.

DØLE TROTTER

Origin: Norway.
Height: Usually a little over 15hh.
Color: As Døle-Gudbrandsdal.
Character: Active, tough, competitive.
Physique (see also Døle-Gudbrandsdal): Hard, active harness horse with a strong look of the Fell pony. Head has a pony or Oriental cast, with open nostrils, pricked ears, and sometimes a concave face. Neck strong, shoulder well-developed and tending to the upright. Roomy chest; body light-framed and well-ribbed-up; hindquarters flexible, long thighs, legs short and iron hard.

The Døle Trotter began more from fashion than from sporting competition. During the 18th century the demand for swift, attractive horse-drawn vehicles reached a peak, justified as it was by practicality as much as by pleasure. The Thoroughbred stallion Odin, imported in 1834, had a lasting effect on the lighter type of Døle horse that has now become the Trotter, and later introductions of trotting blood only added to abilities that were already beginning to appear.

HORSES: COLD BLOODED

NORTH SWEDISH

Origin: Sweden.
Height: 15.1–15.3hh.
Color: Black, bay, brown, chestnut, dun.
Character: Active, willing, extremely good-natured.
Physique: Head rather large with straight face and long ears, in some cases reminiscent of the original Forest type of Northern Europe. Short, crested neck, sturdy, sloping shoulder and roomy chest. Long, deep body, broad and powerful. Round hindquarters with sloping croup. Excellent legs, short and clean and with abundant bone. Large, round feet. Thick mane and tail. Moderate feather on heels. The general effect is of a strong-framed, long-bodied, muscular horse. It is frugal, long-lived, and of excellent constitution. Action is clean, energetic and long-striding.

The North Swedish horse stems from a smaller native horse. Like most native domestic horses of all nations which were not of outstanding appearance, it was for centuries interbred indiscriminately with any available stallion. No distinct type was aimed at until 1890, when a breed society was formed and Døle-Gudbrandsdal stallions, which must be of the same basic stock, were introduced to provide uniformity. Since 1924, North Swedish horses have had their own stud book.

This horse is exceptionally tractable and kind, does well on almost any fare, and is resistant to most diseases. It is thus an economic horse to handle in terms of labor, creating little extra work. It is valued by farmers and timbermen, and has worked well as an artillery horse for the army.

NORTH SWEDISH TROTTER

Origin: Sweden.
Height: 15.1–15.3hh.
Color: Black, bay, brown, chestnut, dun.
Character: Willing, energetic, good-natured.
Physique: Medium head with a straight face. Short, crested neck, sturdy, sloping shoulder and roomy chest. Long, deep body, broad and powerful. Round hindquarters with sloping croup. Excellent, hard legs, short and clean with abundant bone. Round feet. Thick mane and tail. Moderate feather on heels.

For basic information, see North Swedish – the Trotter is of the same breed. The North Swedish horse is a brilliant natural trotter, with an inspiring length of stride and an energetic nature. It is thus to be expected that owners of the fastest animals have been tempted onto the racetrack, and racing with these horses has long been popular in the north of Sweden. The most successful trotters have been selectively interbred for this purpose, and are usually of a somewhat lighter type.

  The North Swedish Trotter cannot compete for speed with the trotter of the European and American tracks.

JUTLAND

Origin: Denmark – Jutland Island.
Height: 15.2–16hh.
Color: Usually chestnut, roan; occasionally bay, black.
Character: Kind, gentle; very easy to handle.
Physique: Typical heavy draught horse; massive, with short legs. Plain head with kind eye, long ears, general expression of gentleness. Short, crested neck. Massive shoulder and front, deep chest; exceptional depth of girth, which exceeds length of leg. Long body, broad and stout, with powerful quarters. Short legs with feather.

This breed seems to have existed for more than a thousand years. There is evidence that it was ridden by the Vikings, and it was certainly the Danish war horse of the Middle Ages. It owes much to the Suffolk Punch, which was imported and crossed with it; and a dubious debt is due to the Yorkshire Coach Horse, which was introduced in the 19th century but did little to improve the breed.

FINNISH

Origin: Finland.
Height: About 15.2hh.
Color: Usually chestnut; also bay, brown, black.
Character: Excellent temperament – at once kind, gentle and very quiet, yet gay and willing.

North Swedish Trotter

Jutland

Physique: Medium head with kind eye and prick ears on short, strong neck. Hard, somewhat upright, shoulder, good chest, deep girth. A round barrel with broad, strong loins and quarters. Legs short and well-proportioned, with good bone and short pasterns. Light feather on heels. Thick mane and tail. A robust, long-lived horse with a straight action. Excellent trotter.

Priority in Finland has traditionally been given to judging a horse by its performance, regardless of its appearance or its breeding. The Finnish horse that has evolved by means of this attitude is an all-rounder with very special qualities of strength, speed, courage, stamina and sweet nature. It is used for hauling timber, as an all-purpose farm horse, competes in trotting races (trotters are specially bred), and makes a quiet and pleasant ride.

It is descended from two closely-related breeds, the Finnish Universal and the Finnish Draught, which have now merged into one. These Finnish breeds were derived from a mixture of many warm- and cold-blood imports which were crossed with the indigenous forest pony.

The Finnish horse possesses characteristics of both warm-blood and cold-blood breeds.

ARDENNAIS

Origin: France and Belgium — Ardennes.
Height: About 15.3hh.
Color: Bay, roan, chestnut.
Character: Very calm and gentle; willing. A child could handle it.
Physique: Massive, compact horse with an immense, muscular frame on short legs. Strong head with a broad face; hugely-crested neck; enormous chest, both in width and depth; near-circular barrel; vast hindquarters — the whole set on short legs of gigantic proportion, especially in the hocks. Abundant feather. Extremely strong. *NB* Ardennais horses reared on poor fare are noticeably lighter in bone and muscle.

This horse is thought to be the horse praised by Caesar in *De Bello Gallico* — but it is impossible to know how much mixing of breed it has undergone since then, or how much wishful thinking there is in identifying it with the willing work-horse of 2,000 years ago. It seems certain that it played an instrumental part in the blood of the Great Horses of the Middle Ages, that it contains Oriental and Belgian blood, that it was used by Napoleon to haul his artillery, and that it experienced a period of work as a coach horse (when it was doubtless not such a heavy animal).

Its enormous services to agriculture and its value to the export trade of France and Belgium have unfortunately been drastically reduced by mechanization, and like so many cold-blooded breeds the Ardennais is on the decline.

Ardennais

SWEDISH ARDENNES

Origin: Sweden.
Height: 15.2–16hh.
Color: Black, bay, brown, chestnut.
Character: Energetic, quiet, kindly.
Physique: Heavy draught horse similar to Ardennais, having a crested neck, immense, muscular body compactly put together, deep girth, and short legs. Not much feather on legs.

The Swedish Ardennes is bred from Ardennais horses imported from Belgium and crossed with the indigenous North Swedish horse, the Ardennais blood being predominant as can be seen from its appearance. The climate and terrain of the Swedish plainlands are sufficiently similar to the Belgian country to have caused little divergence of type from the original imported horses, although when bred in the colder and steeper hill country the horse becomes smaller and more agile.

Formerly much in demand as a carthorse and general heavy farm worker, the Swedish Ardennes is now declining in numbers because of the few tasks that are left for it to do. Its principal use is for timber-hauling in forest areas inaccessible to heavy machinery.

TRAIT DU NORD

Origin: France.
Height: About 16hh.
Color: Bay, chestnut, roan.
Character: Very gentle and docile.
Physique: Very strong heavy draught horse, weighing approximately 1 ton. Similar to the Ardennais in appearance, though bigger and heavier. Has a heavy head and massive neck, a particularly powerful front; deep girth, a muscular body, and strong hindquarters with sloping croup and low-set tail. Feather not excessive for a horse of its type. Very hardy.

The Trait du Nord is a 19th-century offshoot of the Ardennais, bred in the same area of north-east France. It contains additions of Belgian and Dutch Draught blood. The breed was fixed shortly after the turn of the century, and a stud book was opened in 1919.

AUXOIS

Origin: France – Burgundy.
Height: 15.2–16hh.
Color: Red roan or bay.
Character: Quiet, kind, gentle, willing.
Physique: Strong heavy draught horse, similar to Trait du Nord and Ardennais. Large head with longish ears and a general air of kindliness; short, strong neck; massive front; powerful body with deep girth; strong hindquarters with sloping croup and low-set tail. Strong legs with comparatively little feather for a horse of its type. Hardy and enduring.

The Auxois is the old heavy horse of north-eastern Burgundy. It has existed since at least the Middle Ages, and seems originally to have been a somewhat smaller and lighter breed. It was used to pull coaches and was also valued as a draught horse.

More modern methods of farming and the quantity of heavy work triggered by the Industrial Revolution called for a stronger, heavier type of horse, and 19th-century breeders of the Auxois began to cross their mares to Percheron and Boulonnais stallions. Subsequently the Ardennais became the preferred cross and today's Auxois carries much Ardennais blood. The breed is now carefully controlled for type and color.

BRABANT (BELGIAN HEAVY DRAUGHT)

Origin: Belgium – Brabant.
Height: Up to 17hh.
Color: Traditionally red roan with black points, chestnut; sometimes bay, brown, dun, gray.
Character: Bold, energetic horse, willing and good-tempered.

Physique: Powerful horse, tall and massive and compact. Square head, relatively small for its bulk, with intelligent eye and expression of alertness; strong, crested neck; massive shoulders, front, and hindquarters; short back, deep girth, and powerful body. Legs short and muscular, with medium feather. A handsome horse, with great presence and good action. Immensely strong.

This imposing horse, which has had tremendous influence on cold-blooded breeds all over the world, has a history of high romance which is unfortunately not backed up by indisputable evidence. It is said variously that the Brabant is a descendant of the large horse of the Quarternary period, or that it is a descendant of the Ardennais, or both (both are quite possible). It is also said that the Brabant was employed by Caesar (compare Ardennais, page 196), and that it was a medieval Great Horse, which was certainly true of its ancestors, even though the Great Horse of Belgium might not closely resemble the Brabant of today. War horses were bred in both Brabant and Flanders during the Middle Ages and were probably closely related if not identical, though it is the name "Flanders Horse" that occurs most often in history books. There is no horse of that name today.

In the centuries following the Reformation some attempt was made to alter the Brabant by the introduction of various foreign bloodlines, but as this was not considered to effect improvement Belgian breeders soon began

Brabant (Belgian Heavy Draught)

to work only with pure Brabant strains, and thus a breed was established whose pedigree is of some antiquity. Selective breeding was practised with great diligence, even to the extent of close inbreeding for outstanding qualities. As a result, the Brabant of today is a magnificent animal which invariably breeds true.

DUTCH DRAUGHT

Origin: Holland.
Height: Up to 16.3hh.
Color: Chestnut, bay, gray; occasionally black.
Character: Quiet and very kind, yet active, spirited and bold. A hard worker.
Physique: Tall, massive horse of good conformation, hard and deep. Good head with straight face, intelligent eye, and short, alert ears; short neck; powerful front, withers slight; deep girth, body massive and close to the ground; heavily-muscled loins and hindquarters; short, muscular legs, good feet. Action straight and easy. Carries itself well. Extremely strong, with boundless stamina.

This heavy draught horse is largely of Belgian blood. The breed is not much more than a half-century old, and was created from the old Zeeland horse, a very similar sort to the Brabant, crossed mainly with Ardennais blood and to a lesser extent that of the Ardennais. Quality and purity of line has been, and still is, supervised with great care, and a special stud book exists for horses which have achieved a high standard of physical excellence at maturity.

PERCHERON

Origin: France – Perche region (specifically, the Departments Sarthe, Eure-et-Loire, Loire-et-Cher, L'Orne).
Height: 15.2–17hh.
Color: Gray, black.
Character: Energetic, intelligent, docile, easy to handle.
Physique: Fine head with straight face, wide-spaced, intelligent eyes, open nostrils; strong, crested neck; powerful front with deep chest; deep, close-coupled body with strong loins; round, immensely-strong hindquarters. Medium-short legs, hard and muscular and almost devoid of feather. Excellent action, great poise and presence. Despite its size, huge frame, and massive strength, the Percheron has a cast of Oriental grace.

The elegance of the Percheron, surprising in so heavy a breed, has caused it to be likened to an overgrown Arab; and indeed some of its ancestors were Arabians. It stems from Oriental and Norman horses, mixed many centuries ago and later crossed with heavy draught breeds, apparently seasoned again with a little extra Arab.

Percheron

It has been distributed all over the world, and wherever it is bred it arouses great enthusiasm and profound attention to quality and purity of line. In France, the true Percheron is allowed only if it is bred in one of the four Departments (listed above) of its native region of Perche. The other Percheron types – the Auge, Berry, Loire, Maine and Nivernais – are not included in the Percheron stud book and have separate stud books of their own. In North America, to which it was first exported in 1839, it has attracted many sincere admirers and the strictest attention has been and is paid to the production of a perfect type. In Great Britain the Percheron has been bred to exclude all feather from its feet, and is much used as a cross with the Thoroughbred to produce the perfect type of heavyweight hunter.

The Percheron is a rugged, active horse, intelligent and charming. It is easy to handle, economic to keep, and of sound constitution. It is an attractive mover, poised and balanced. It is the most popular carthorse in the world.

BOULONNAIS

Origin: France (Northern).
Height: 16–16.3hh.
Color: Usually gray; sometimes chestnut, bay.
Character: Lively, intelligent, good-natured.
Physique: Elegant heavy draught horse, very similar to the Percheron in

appearance. Fine head with a straight or slightly-concave face, faintly reminiscent of the Arab; small ears. Strong neck; deep, powerful body with ample front and hindquarters, pronounced dip in the back. Short, muscular legs with big joints and little feather. Bushy mane and silky coat. General effect is of grace and harmony.

Like the Percheron, the Boulonnais has Oriental blood. This, together with an Andalusian strain introduced during the Middle Ages, accounts for its noble appearance. Its strength and size come from the old Great Horses of Northern Europe. A horse that is easy to admire, it both fills the eye and fulfils its function as an active, hard-working farm horse.

BRETON

Origin: France — Brittany.
Height: 14.3–16hh.
Color: Red roan, blue roan, chestnut, bay; black very rare.
Character: Lively, attractive horse, active, willing, sweet-tempered.
Physique: Three types exist:
> *Draught Breton:* Dense, compact heavy draught horse with attractive head, short, crested neck, deep, powerful body, and short legs with pronounced joints and very little feather;
> *Postier Breton:* Medium-weight coach/draught horse standing not much over 15hh, strong and solid, having excellent, clearly-defined action, especially at the trot;
> *Corlay:* Coach or saddle horse standing 14.3–15.1hh.
> The type shown in the illustration is a Draught Breton.

The indigenous horse of north-western France, though developed along separate lines, is still known under the single heading of Breton. Crossed with Percheron, Ardennais and Boulonnais breeds it has given rise to the Draught Breton, while the smart action and lighter build of the Postier Breton is due to Norfolk Trotter and Hackney blood. The lightweight Corlay horse, now almost extinct, is the product of crosses with Thoroughbred and Arab.

COMTOIS

Origin: France — Franche-Comté.
Height: 14.3–15.3hh.
Color: Solid colors — bay is commonest, then chestnut.
Character: Courageous, active, kind and willing.
Physique: Light draught horse with large head, straight neck, good front and withers. Girth deep, back long and straight, hindquarters strong; legs well-made with good bone, though showing a tendency to sickle hocks. Feather is comparatively light, mane and tail thick. Hardy and sure-footed.

Reared in the rugged hill country of the Franco-Swiss borderland, this

Boulonnais

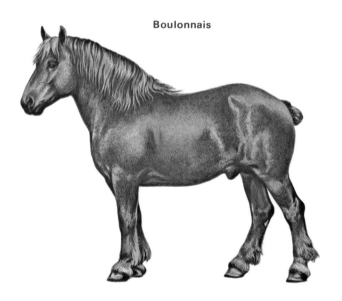

Breton

horse has developed a quick and lively action unusual in a heavy breed. Like all mountain horses it is sure-footed and active, and it is no doubt owing to the combination of these qualities with its strength and good disposition that it was valued as a military horse from the Middle Ages onwards. It is said to have been brought to the Franche-Comté region as early as the 6th century.

POITEVIN

Origin: France — Poitou.
Height: 16.2–17hh.
Color: Usually dun. Can be bay, brown.
Character: Sober, dull, lethargic.
Physique: Large, gaunt horse, undistinguished and usually unattractive. Heavy head with long, thick ears; short, straight neck; powerful, but often upright, shoulder; inadequate depth of girth for its size and weight; long body; strong, sloping hindquarters; massive legs with heavy feather, very large feet.

This plain, thick-witted horse was originally imported from the flatlands of Northern Europe to drain the marshes round Poitiers, a job for which it was particularly qualified by virtue of its enormous feet. It might have died out long ago had it not possessed one very special quality: it produces excellent mules. Poitevin horses are bred to produce Poitevin mares, the best of whom in turn are bred to tall jackasses of the *baudet Poitevin* strain. The resulting large mules are valuable.

ITALIAN HEAVY DRAUGHT

Origin: Italy — northern and central areas.
Height: 15–16hh.
Color: Classic color is dark liver chestnut with chestnut/blond mane and tail; also chestnut, roan.
Character: Active, willing, lively horse, though kind and docile.
Physique: Heavy draught horse. Fine, rather long head with tapering muzzle, medium-long ears, alert expression; short, crested neck, often convex on the underside; powerful shoulder, deep broad chest, little or no withers; deep girth, compact, robust body with broad, flat back and strong loins; round, powerful hindquarters; hard legs with pronounced joints and moderate feather; boxy feet.

The unusual, striking color of this horse combined with its quick and energetic action make it a pleasure to watch. It stems from the Breton horse, and has been much appreciated in Italy as a strong and willing worker on the farms. Unfortunately, mechanization has largely outmoded it, and today it is bred more for the slaughterhouse than for the farm.

Poitevin

Italian Heavy Draught

RHINELAND HEAVY DRAUGHT

Origin: West Germany.
Height: 16–17hh.
Color: Chestnut, red roan with blond mane and tail, red roan with black points.
Character: Good-natured, obliging animal which matures early.
Physique: Massive, bulky horse of enormous power. Relatively neat head with kind eye and open nostril; strong, crested neck; massive, muscular shoulders and hindquarters; body dense, deep-girthed, with broad back and powerful loins; legs muscular and short, with medium feather.

The Rhineland, or Rhenish, horse was developed towards the end of the 19th century to meet a growing demand from agriculture and industry. By the early 20th century it had become the most numerous of all the German breeds and was bred all over the country, often going under a variety of local names. Today it and its offshoots are fast dying out from lack of demand. One of the very few Rhineland types to exist nowadays is the Niedersachen Heavy Draught.

SCHLESWIG HEAVY DRAUGHT

Origin: Germany – Schleswig-Holstein.
Height: 15.2–16hh.
Color: Almost always chestnut, often with flaxen mane and tail; occasionally gray, bay.
Character: Kind, gentle, willing.
Physique: Compact, dense horse. Plain, rather large head with convex profile and kind eye. Short, crested neck; powerful front with broad chest, deep girth, withers almost unnoticeable. Body rather long and slab-sided. Short, muscular legs, lightly-feathered. Good mover.

This breed is similar to the Jutland, to which it is closely related, and to the Suffolk Punch, though it is a shade lighter and more cob-like than either. Bred, like the Rhineland, to satisfy a 19th-century demand for a strong agricultural and industrial worker of good temperament, it contains a variety of bloodlines. It derives largely from Jutland and Suffolk horses, helped by Breton and Boulonnais blood. Even the Thoroughbred and Yorkshire Coach Horse had small parts to play in its history, though their influence is not noticeable.

PINZGAUER NORIKER

Origin: Austria and Germany.
Height: 16–16.2hh.
Color: Predominantly bay, chestnut (often with flaxen mane and tail); also spotted, dun, skewbald.
Character: Alert, active, docile.

Rhineland Heavy Draught

Pinzgauer Noriker

Physique: Plain, heavy head with gentle expression; short, thick neck; powerful, rather upright shoulder, large chest; long barrel with broad back; good hindquarters. Legs are medium-short with pronounced joints and little feather. Good feet. Very sure-footed and moves well.

This ancient breed of horse is said to have been bred under Roman rule in the Kingdom of Noricum, which covered roughly the same area as Austria does today. "Pinzgauer" refers to the Pinzgau district of Austria. About the time of the Renaissance the Church took an interest in its development and enriched it with Andalusian and Neapolitan blood.

Bred as it has long been in the mountains, the Noriker is adapted to steep hill country in a way that few heavy breeds can match. For this reason it is still in demand in central and southern Europe, and is said even to be on the increase.

It is also known as the South German Cold-Blood.

MURAKOZ

Origin: Hungary.
Height: About 16hh.
Color: Usually chestnut, often with flaxen mane and tail; also bay, brown, gray, black.
Character: Docile, willing, active.
Physique: Plain, neat head with convex face, kind eye, large ears. Neck short and lightly-crested. Very powerful front, almost no withers, deep girth; strong body of medium length with pronounced dip in back; rounded hindquarters with sloping croup. Short, muscular legs with pronounced joints and medium/light feather. Round feet.

Bred in the south of Hungary on the banks of the river Mura, the Muraköz is a selective blend of native mares with quality Hungarian stallions, Ardennais, Percherons and Norikers. It is a strong, active horse, well fitted to heavy farm work, and it met the Hungarian need so well that shortly after the First World War one out of every five horses in the land was a Muraköz. Many were killed during World War II, and it is now most unlikely that it will ever regain its former numbers.

RUSSIAN HEAVY DRAUGHT

Origin: USSR — Ukraine.
Height: Averagely just over 14.2hh.
Color: Solid colors — mostly chestnut, roan, bay.
Character: Very pleasant nature — sweet-tempered and lively.
Physique: Smallest of the heavy draught breeds, dense and compact. Medium-small, alert head with bright, kind eye and pricked ears; massive neck and front, flat withers; good depth of girth, hard, round barrel, and broad back with pronounced dip; sloping croup, strong hindquarters. Legs short with little feather, hard hooves. Action light, free and quick.

Murakoz

Russian Heavy Draught

This small, attractive horse is another Russian development of the last hundred years. It was achieved by crossing Swedish Ardennes, Percherons and Orlov Trotters onto indigenous cart mares of the Ukraine breed.

The Russian Heavy Draught has the power to haul huge loads, and works fast and well. It is employed on collective farms throughout much of western Russia.

LITHUANIAN HEAVY DRAUGHT

Origin: USSR — Baltic States.
Height: 15—15.3hh.
Color: Usually chestnut, often with flaxen mane and tail; also black, bay, roan, gray.
Character: Placid to the point of indolence. Good worker.
Physique: A massive, handsome horse with a medium-sized, fine head. The neck is short and crested; shoulders and hindquarters massive; body long, deep and dense, with a pronounced dip in the back; sloping, bifurcated croup. Legs are short and of dense bone, with very little feather. Tendency to sickle hocks. Action free and straight.

There are two types of Lithuanian, the Basic and the Lighter. The latter, as its name implies, is lighter-framed. It is also taller.

The Lithuanian Heavy Draught horse is the result of nearly a century of selective breeding for performance of progeny of the smaller, more active Zhmud horse of Lithuania with Swedish Ardennes imports. The new breed, a consistently effective draught horse, was first registered in 1963.

VLADIMIR HEAVY DRAUGHT

Origin: USSR.
Height: About 16hh.
Color: Any solid color.
Character: Energetic, competitive, hard-working.
Physique: Strong work horse of good conformation. Small head with convex profile and alert expression; medium-length, crested neck, set well on powerful shoulders, good chest; strong, medium-length body with slight dip in back; stout loins and hindquarters; strong legs with heavy feather.

English blood, especially that of the Shire horse, is at once apparent from the appearance of the Vladimir Heavy Draught. The breed was founded during the latter part of the 19th century, using a mixture of Suffolk Punch, Cleveland Bay, Ardennais and Percheron. Shire blood was first introduced in 1910 and was continued until shortly after World War I, when interbreed crossing was stopped and selective inbreeding between the best of the progeny became the exclusive practice. By 1946 a horse of great strength and all-round usefulness had emerged, having also the ability to breed true. At this point the breed was considered fixed.

Vladimir Heavy Draught

SUFFOLK PUNCH

Origin: England – East Anglia.
Height: Around 16–16.2hh.
Color: Exclusively chestnut. Seven shades exist – red, gold, copper, yellow, liver, light, dark. No white markings, though faint star or stripe is sometimes apparent.
Character: Kind, honest, intelligent, active.
Physique: Dense, compact heavy draught horse with short, clean legs. Short, attractive head with kind eye, well-set on a muscular, crested neck. Massive shoulder with deep, wide chest, flat withers; deep girth, body dense and almost cylindrical, with broad, strong back and round and powerful hindquarters. Dense, clean legs with good bone, short cannon bones and pasterns; no feather. Good action in all paces, but especially at the trot. Long-lived, hardy, and an economical feeder.

The Suffolk Punch is one of the purest of all breeds of heavy horse. It seems to have arisen quite naturally from local animals of the Great Horse type, Norfolk Trotters, Norfolk Cobs, with possibly a touch of Thoroughbred. It was mentioned as early as 1506, and from about the turn of the 18th/19th century seems to have been carefully and selectively bred. All Suffolk horses trace back to a smallish chestnut trotting horse called Blakes Farmer, who was foaled in 1760.

It is a deservedly popular animal. It has excellent conformation, a gentle and charming disposition, and it comes to hand early and can work until well on in its twenties. Though its great service to agriculture is regrettably becoming a thing of the past, its presence and personality ensure that it will continue to attract enthusiasts who want to preserve it for its own sake.

CLYDESDALE

Origin: Scotland – Lanarkshire.
Height: Average 16.2hh.
Color: Bay, brown, black, roan, with much white on the face and legs and sometimes on the body. Bay and brown are the commonest colors.
Character: Active, brave and friendly.
Physique: Broad, flat face, neither dished nor roman, wide muzzle with large nostrils, clear, intelligent eyes. Long, well-arched neck, high withers; short, strong back setting into heavily-muscled hindquarters. Forelegs straight and directly under shoulder, hind legs also straight. Much feather, covering long pasterns and hard feet. Action straight with a long, free stride, feet picked up cleanly with the inside of every hoof visible to anyone walking behind. Active movers for their bulk.

Clydesdales originate from Lanarkshire, the Lowland county through which the Clyde runs (the old name for Lanarkshire was Clydesdale). In the mid-18th century development of the Lanarkshire coalfields led to a great improvement in road surfaces, so that shoulder-haulage by horses could be substituted for pack carrying. Local farmers, anxious to profit from the need for heavier, stronger horses to pull the loads, crossed their hardy native mares with much heavier Flemish stallions, which were imported for this purpose. They named the result the Clydesdale.

The new breed quickly became popular, and has been a regular export from the British Isles for more than a century, going wherever horses were required for haulage. In 1911 a Clydesdale established a British record for heavy horse prices when the stallion Baron of Buchlyvie was sold at auction for £9,500.

SHIRE

Origin: England – Central counties (Shires).
Height: Average 17hh. Can reach, and even exceed, 18hh.
Color: Bay and brown are commonest, always with white markings; black and gray are not unusual.
Character: A gentle, docile horse, so kind that it can usually be trusted with a child; active, industrious, adaptable, enduring.
Physique: Medium-sized head of delicate proportion, faintly-convex profile, kind eye, broad forehead, long, slender ears. Neck long and arched, well-set on powerful, sloping shoulders with a deep front. Body dense and rounded; back broad with strong loins; hindquarters full and powerful, often with sloping croup. Excellent legs, long for a heavy horse, with dense

Suffolk Punch

Clydesdale

bone. Abundant feather, fine and silky. Possesses great strength and stamina and is of sound constitution.

This controversial horse — controversial in the sense that it attracts enthusiasts, and enthusiasts attract argument — has a grand, although none-too-precise history. It derives from the Old English Black Horse, which in turn stems from the Great Horse of chivalric times. The Great Horse's ancestry is uncertain, but it is likely to have come from northern European stock, especially from the black Friesian horses. The extreme height of the Shire may be partly due to Thoroughbred blood, which would also account for its aristocratic appearance.

When the demand for war horses ceased and the need for strong agricultural animals became apparent, breeders were quick to recognize and improve the merits of the Shire. Standards of quality were established early on, records were kept, and in 1878 the Shire Horse Society was established.

With mechanization, demand for the Shire declined. Its continued existence is ensured by its popularity as a team horse to pull brewers' drays (now mainly ornamental) as well as its ability to draw crowds to the show ring. It is a horse that breeds true, it is a pleasure to work with; and though its great strength is no longer needed — it can pull five tons — it will always be welcome.

It is the tallest horse in the world.

Shire

HORSE TYPES

COB

This is a sturdy, placid animal of the type known in Medieval times as a *rouncy* or *roncey*. Its breeding is largely a matter of chance – often it is the by-product of an attempt to produce a heavyweight hunter from a part-bred cart mare crossed with a quality stallion, sometimes resulting even when the stallion is a Thoroughbred and the mare herself no more than a heavyweight hunter.

The ideal cob stands from 14.2 to 15.2hh, has a quality head on a thick-crested neck, strong, sloping shoulders, a short back with a deep girth, generous, rounded hindquarters with second thighs, short legs with abundant bone and very short cannon bones, and hard, round feet. It has a calm, intelligent expression, and may be any color. Its action should be long-striding and smooth and very comfortable.

The cob is generally thought of as a perfect ride for the elderly and the obese. As such, its manners must be perfect – safe, calm, obedient and comfortable. It is extremely strong, ideal for a heavy rider who wants a hard day's hunting on sticky ground, but its lack of speed prevents it from rivalling the heavy hunter on fast grassland countries. Its unruffleable temperament creates a demand for it in many situations where a high-strung horse would be worse than useless – for example, that of a racehorse trainer who has to supervise a string of nervous young Thoroughbreds. It is a sort of horse which has been, and will be, appreciated for a very long time.

HACK

The name of this horse stems from the once-despised *hackney* or *haquenai* (see page 100). It is, as it has always been, a riding horse; but it has risen in caste from the humble hireling of Medieval times, through a period when it was the mount of a gentleman galloping to a meet of foxhounds (the groom going slowly on ahead on the gentleman's hunter), to a meaning which is generally associated with any high-class small Thoroughbred or quality riding horse. It should not be overlooked that "going for a hack" means going out riding purely for pleasure, as opposed to going hunting or to some other sporting event, and that any horse which provides an enjoyable ride may justifiably be described as a hack. It is required to have good manners, pleasant gaits, and an ability to negotiate small fences.

In the show rings of the world the hack is also required to have great personal beauty. Because of this, European prizes usually fall to the small Thoroughbred and in America preponderantly to the Saddlebred. Show standards require the hack to be not more than 15.3hh, to be of perfect conformation, elegant carriage and appearance, to have a smooth, true action, and to be possessed of perfect manners. It may be of any color, as befits a type rather than a breed, but because of its "breedy" appearance is usually to be found in the conventional solid colors of bay, brown, black, gray or chestnut. Its lightweight build – in show ring terms it is always a lightweight – especially fits it as a woman's mount.

SHOW PONY

Literally, an animal standing not more than 14.2hh and having conformation good enough to win in the show ring. Show ponies come in three sizes – up to 12.2hh, up to 13.2hh, and up to 14.2hh. They are judged on conformation, manners, action at the walk, trot and canter (they are not usually required to jump), and some consideration is also given to the way in which they are turned out, presented, and ridden.

In a big horse show there will always be a number of ponies who will be faultless or near-faultless. Emphasis therefore shifts to their performance. The usual method of selection is for all ponies to parade around the show ring at a walk, trot and canter. Those that catch the judge's eye are called into the center of the ring and lined up to wait until this initial selection process has been completed. When the rank and file has been dismissed the selected ponies who remain are put through their paces one by one, performing at the walk, collected and extended trot, and collected and extended canter. Some display of elementary dressage is usually required. The judge will inspect each pony from all angles, and will usually run his hand over its body and down its legs. At this halfway stage the best ponies are moved into the front of two ranks, and from then on in it becomes a battle of nerves (for the rider) while the judge considers minute details.

As the object is to select the perfect child's pony, color and breed are not material. A show pony can come from any background; but since it must be both elegant and conventionally good-looking to reach the top it is usually, though not necessarily, a small Thoroughbred or near-Thoroughbred.

Cob

Hack

As long as it can and will jump formidable obstacles in cold blood, a show jumper can be any size, color, breed or height. Successful ones must be bold, brave, disciplined and must have tremendous power of thrust. In many competitions, speed is also a factor. Show jumpers must also be handy, able to cope with sharp turns and difficult approaches to fences, and must possess nerves equal to the strain of competition and resilient to the noise and electricity generated by an excited crowd. The best of them love an audience, responding visibility to the oohs and aahs of suspense as they clear each jump.

Top class show jumpers command prices far in excess of anything they can ever be expected to win in prize money, and as such are the prerogative of the luxury market. Often they provide a hobby (but a very serious one) for those who can comfortably afford not only the purchase price but the high cost, in the cases of the best horses, of international travel, and horses of this caliber are frequently not owner-ridden but are piloted by the cream of the amateur and professional riders.

Good show jumpers are distinguished by compactness of build and by the tremendous power of their hindquarters. Most are mongrels who show an aptitude for jumping, though such as Hanoverians, Irish horses and hunters are conspicuous in the top ranks. In 1902 the North American hunter Heatherbloom cleared the astonishing height of 8ft 3in.

Show Jumper

Hunter

HUNTER

A hunter is simply any horse which is suited to foxhunting. As such, it must be bold, intelligent and tractable, capable of negiotiating all kinds of obstacle which come in its path and sound enough in wind and limb to last for up to 5 hours at a trot and gallop without tiring.

Hunters vary according to the type of country hunted. In heavy going, a strong-built horse will endure the exhausting suck of plough which will cause a lightweight horse to stagger and quickly tire. On fast grassland, a Thoroughbred or other lightweight animal will sweep past the slow-footed heavy horses. In trappy country a courageous and resourceful horse will prove to be the best. Variations exist also according to the weight and strength of the rider, since there is no point in the chase if the horse cannot carry you, and no point also if the horse is so strong that he carries you past the Master and into the pack of hounds.

The essential qualities of a hunter are soundness, endurance, intelligence, jumping ability, good manners, an equable temperament, and stamina. In the show ring, hunters are judged on appearance, good behavior and comfortable action. Show hunters are divided into 5 categories according to weight: up to 175lb (lightweight), up to 196 (middleweight), over 196 (heavyweight), small (14.2–15.2hh), and ladies'. The classic type of hunter – the famous Irish horse – is a cross between a Thoroughbred and an Irish Draught or Cleveland Bay mare, brought on slowly on good land.

RACEHORSE

Though the word "racehorse" has become synonymous with the word "Thoroughbred" it does not necessarily follow that Thoroughbreds are the only horses which are raced. Testing horses against each other for speed has been known to exist for more than 5,000 years, or for 4,800—4,900 years before the Thoroughbred was evolved, and it is likely that races were held for many centuries or millenia before this. Very early forms of racing are thought to have involved restricting horses from water until they were extremely thirsty and then loosing them to see which would get to the water first. Wherever and whenever man had a horse he was proud of, or simply whenever he felt like a gamble, races have been held, be it Roman chariot racing, a private match between gentlemen, steeplechasing, trotting racing, or any other form of speed or endurance contest that could be imagined.

Modern-day racing includes such widely-diverse forms as speed tests for Arabs, for Shetland ponies (in North America), and for sulky trotters. In a sense, all of these animals qualify for the description of racing horses or ponies; but it is to the Thoroughbred alone, with its unique turn of foot, that the title of "racehorse" truly belongs.

Thoroughbreds are raced the world over. The standard of their performances varies quite strongly from country to country, since performance of horse versus horse and not horse versus clock is what matters, and thus rejects from a good racing nation often become winners in a weak one.

POLO PONY

Polo ponies are not usually bred as such, but are picked out as young adults if they show an aptitude for the game. They need to stand around 15hh or a little over — not "ponies" at all in the strict sense of the word — and they must be fast, bold, intelligent and extremely handy. Most are of near or pure Thoroughbred ancestry. Training them takes a good deal of time and patience.

The origins of polo are obscure. It seems to have been played in eastern Asia for many centuries, and to have lost its popularity in such countries as China and Mongolia only comparatively recently. Western enthusiasm for the game came about through its discovery by English tea planters in Assam a little more than a century ago (see Manipur pony, page 72). The Silchar Club, founded in 1859 in Assam, is the oldest polo club in the world, and its rules provided the basis for modern polo.

It is a game well suited to regimental life, and many of its successful participants have consistently been army officers. Spreading back with the British regiments from India to England, it quickly (1870s) found a home at the Hurlingham Club. From there it was successfully taken up in the United States, and since 1945 the North American supremacy has been overcome by that of Argentina.

Today, most of the world's polo ponies are bred in Argentina, which has roughly three times as many polo players as any other nation in the world.

INDEX

Page numbers in italics refer to illustrations.